TEACH YOURSELF BOOKS

SPANISH
VOCABULARY

A COMPLETE LEARNING TOOL

SPANISH VOCABULARY

A COMPLETE LEARNING TOOL

Series Editor: Rosi McNab

Language Editor: Pilar Caldeiro López

TEACH YOURSELF BOOKS

For UK orders: please contact Bookpoint Ltd, 130 Milton Park, Abingdon, Oxon OX14 4SB. Telephone: (44) 01235 827720, Fax: (44) 01235 400454. Lines are open from 09.00–18.00, Monday to Saturday, with a 24-hour message answering service. You can also order through our website www.madaboutbooks.com

For U.S.A. order enquiries: please contact McGraw-Hill Customer Services, P.O. Box 545, Blacklick, OH 43004-0545, U.S.A. Telephone 1-800-722-4726. Fax: 1-614-755-5645.

For Canada order enquiries: please contact McGraw-Hill Ryerson Ltd., 300 Water St, Whitby, Ontario L1N 9B6, Canada. Telephone: 905 430 5000. Fax: 905 430 5020.

Long renowned as the authoritative source for self-guided learning – with more than 30 million copies sold worldwide – the *Teach Yourself* series includes over 300 titles in the fields of languages, crafts, hobbies, business and education.

British Library Cataloguing in Publication Data
A catalogue record for this title is available from The British Library

Library of Congress Catalog Card Number: 95–71314

First published in UK 1996 by Hodder Headline Plc, 338 Euston Road, London NW1 3BH.

First published in US 1996 by Contemporary Books, A Division of The McGraw-Hill Companies, 1 Prudential Plaza, 130 East Randolph Street, Chicago, Illinois 60601 U.S.A.

The 'Teach Yourself' name and logo are registered trade marks of Hodder & Stoughton Ltd.

Typeset by Transet Limited, Coventry, England.
Printed in Great Britain for Hodder & Stoughton Educational, a division of Hodder Headline Ltd, 338 Euston Road, London NW1 3BH by Cox & Wyman Ltd, Reading, Berkshire.

Impression number	18	17	16	15	14	13	12	11
Year		2007	2006	2005	2004	2003	2002	

CONTENTS

INTRODUCTION

──────── **About this book** ────────

This book is an easy-to-use reference book of key language for the language student, business traveller and holidaymaker.

It is designed to be EASY to use, both:
• as a quick reference to find useful words in a specific area, and
• to increase your word power by building up a stock of new vocabulary.

──────── **How to use the book** ────────

The words in each topic are divided into further sub-topics for easy reference, for example within the major topic area of *La casa, el hogar y el jardín* (House, home and garden), you will find amongst other sub-topics *Las partes de la casa* (Parts of the house). Within these sub-topics, the words are further divided into smaller groupings with other words of similar meaning. There are also some examples of how words might be used in a sentence.

──── **Pronunciation of Spanish:** ────
guidelines

Spanish pronunciation is relatively easy to learn as there are fewer different sounds than in English and in general spelling and pronunciation go together. The following guidelines are of course no substitute for first hand exposure to the language, so students should take every opportunity to listen to native speakers and to imitate what they hear.

Introduction

The Spanish alphabet

The Spanish alphabet now has 27 letters, of which 26 are common to English and Spanish. The extra letter is **ñ**.

The Spanish alphabet is therefore:

a	j	r
b	k	s
c	l	t
d	m	u
e	n	v
f	ñ	w
g	o	x
h	p	y
i	q	z

You may find that other books and dictionaries say there are 30 letters in the Spanish alphabet. This is because there are three sounds particular to Spanish: **ch**, **ll**, **rr**. Until recently, all of these were considered as separate letters, although in 1994 it was officially decided that they will no longer be considered as such.

Spanish vowels

Spanish vowels are very pure sounds, and each has only one pronunciation. They are pronounced in a clear, somewhat sharp way and English speakers need to make an effort to give each vowel its own, particular pronunciation, and to avoid the temptation of giving them the unstressed vowel sound which is so common in English (as in words such as not**a**ble, p**e**ncil, Lond**o**n).

a   slightly longer than the 'a' of 'cat'
mañana; **Salamanca**; **para**
Note that in the first example, the three **a**'s all have the same "clear" pronunciation. Do not pronounce the second **a** 'ar', as in 'car'.

e   similar to the 'e' in 'get'
Enrique; **Benavente**; **empresa**

Introduction

i   like the 'ee' in 'seen'
fino; rico
a 'y' at the end of the word is pronounced in the same way:
rey; ley
o   if the syllable ends in 'o' it is pronounced like the 'o' in 'vote'
poco; bravo; esto
if the syllable ends in a consonant, it has a shorter pronunciation, like the 'o' in 'off'
sol; costa
u   like the 'oo' in 'pool'
luna; museo; música
Note however that the **u** is silent after **q** and between **g** and **e** or **i**:
Guernica; Miguel; guitarra; guía
unless there are two dots over it:
pingüino; Sigüenza

Diphthongs

When a 'strong' vowel (**a**, **o** or **e**) combines with a 'weak' vowel (**i** or **u**) it is known as a diphthong.

ai/ay   like 'i' in 'hide'
baile; hay
au   like 'ou' in 'found'
causa; bautizo
ei/ey   like 'ay' in 'pay'
reina; ley
ie   like 'ye' in 'yellow'
viejo; cien
oi/oy   like 'oy' in 'toy'
oiga; voy

Spanish Consonants

b, v   have the same sound, similar to an English 'b' but a little softer. The English sound 'v' does not exist in Spanish.
vino; bar; abanico

Introduction

c   like 'th' in 'thick' when followed by **e** or **i**
Barcelona; Valencia; hacer; cerveza
like 'c' in 'car' when followed by **a, o, u** or a consonant
cantar; comer; crimen

ch   like the 'ch' in 'child'
mucho; leche; churro

d   between vowels and after consonants (except **l** and **n**) the 'd' has a very soft pronunciation, like 'th' in 'the'
cada; sidra
at the end of words it has an even softer pronunciation, and is often omitted
usted; ciudad; Madrid
otherwise, it is pronounced like the 'd' in 'date'
día; delante; andar

f   like 'f' in 'four'
café; foto

g   has two pronunciations:
– guttural, like **j**, when it is followed by an **e** or **i**
gitano; general
– as in the English 'gut' when it is followed by **a, o** or **u**
gato; agosto; agua

h   is always silent in Spanish
hotel; hielo; Alhambra

j   has a guttural sound, rather like the Scottish 'ch' in 'loch'
jamón; Rioja; naranja

k   is rare in Spanish. Pronounced like 'k' in 'king'
kilo; Kodak

l   like 'l' in 'like'
Inglaterra, español

ll   like the 'lli' in 'million'
Sevilla; paella; millón

m   like 'm' in 'milk'
mucho; mano

n   like 'n' in 'not'
pan; nada

ñ   This is different to a normal **n**, and is pronounced like the 'ni' in 'onion'.
señor; señorita; España
There are no common words which begin with **ñ**.

p   like 'p' in 'pull' but without an aspiration
       guapo; padre; pescado

q   is always pronounced like 'k' in 'king' and never like the 'qu' in
       'queen'
       quiosco; queso

r   is always "rolled" - with one or two flips of the tip of the tongue
       sombrero; señorita
       At the beginning of a word **r** is pronounced like **rr**.

rr   has an even more noticeable roll than **r**
       ferrocarril; carretera

s   like 's' in 'some'
       casa; sangre; secreto
       except before a 'voiced consonant' (**b, d, g, l, m** and **n**) when it
       is like the 's' in 'hose'
       desde; mismo

t   like 't' in 'tennis' but without an aspiration
       también; taza; patata

v   see the note on 'b'

w   is really only found in English words which have been
       absorbed into the Spanish language. It is pronounced like a **b/v**
       wáter (*lavatory*); **waterpolo;**
       or kept as an English 'w'
       Walkman™; whisky

x   before a vowel, usually like 'ex' in 'excellent' (not 'example')
       máximo
       before a consonant, usually like 's' in 'sad'
       extra; sexto

z   like 'th' in 'thing'
       zapato; zumo; andaluz

Stress Rules

Spanish words are stressed on the last syllable if they end in a
consonant other than **n** or **s**:
español; hablar
They are stressed on the last but one syllable if they end in **n** or **s** or a
vowel:
billete; gasolina; comprenden; muchachas
The majority of Spanish words fall into this category.

Introduction

If a word breaks either of these rules, an accent is written to show where the stress falls:
sábado; **teléfono**; **habitación**
All words ending in **-ión** carry the stress in this way.
So if you see a word with a written accent, you must stress the syllable where the accent is placed. (Failure to do this could result in a misunderstanding.)
An accent is also used to differentiate between words of identical spelling but with different meanings:
si (*if*), **sí** (*yes*); **el** (*the*), **él** (*he*)

Pronunciation practice

Now practise your pronunciation by saying:

1 All the words you can remember from the examples;
2 Then try these:
   La paella es un plato típico de Valencia.
   Dos botellas de vino de Rioja
   Un zumo de naranja
   El rey de España se llama Juan Carlos.
   Un vaso de agua con hielo
   Un billete de ida y vuelta
   ¡Lleno, por favor!
   Sí, hablo español.
   En Madrid, quiero comprar una guitarra y un abanico.
   Una guía de hoteles españoles

——— Vocabulary learning ———

Follow the simple suggestions in this introduction to help you to increase your vocabulary.

There are also *¡Otra vez!* (Once again!) activities with which to test yourself and so make learning easier.

So how can I learn more effectively?

Most people complain of having a poor memory. They say they are no

Introduction

good at learning a language because they can't remember the words, but few people have difficulty in remembering things which really interest them: the names of members of a football team, the parts of a car, what happened in the last episode of a favourite radio or TV series, the ingredients in a recipe ...!

How can I make learning a list of words more interesting?

1 First YOU decide which list you are going to learn today.
2 Then YOU decide which words in that list you want to try to learn.
   Mark each word. (Put a mark beside each word you have chosen.)
   Count them. (How many are you going to try to learn?)
   Underline the first letter of each word. (What letters do they begin with?)
   Now you are ready to begin.
3 Say the words ALOUD. If you put your hands over your ears whilst you read them it will cut out extraneous noise and help you to concentrate by reflecting the sound of your voice and helping you to hear what you sound like. You should have studied the previous section in this introduction on pronunciation before doing this.
4 Next look for ways to learn them. Do you know how YOU learn words best?

Learning

Try this quick test to find out how you learn best:

• Look at the words with translations in *Method 1*, and the illustrated word list in *Method 2* for one minute and try to remember as many words as possible.
• Close the book and write down in Spanish a list of the words you remember.

7

Introduction

Method 1: translated lists

el caballo	*horse*	el zapato	*shoe*
la botella	*bottle*	el plátano	*banana*
el cuchillo	*knife*	el avión	*aeroplane*
el pan	*bread*	la puerta	*gate*
la bufanda	*scarf*	el libro	*book*
la carta	*letter*	la taza	*cup*

Method 2: illustrations

el árbol   la bicicleta   la bombilla   el elefante   la flor   los guantes

el grifo   la manzana   el reloj   la silla   la ventana   el barco

Have you remembered more words from the the group of illustrated words, or or from the word list?

If you have remembered more of the words from the list rather than from the pictures, you have a preference for memorising the written word and you may find it helpful to write down the words you are learning.

If you have remembered more of the illustrated words, this shows you have a more visual memory. You will probably find it helpful to 'tie in' the words you learn to a quick drawing.

If you didn't remember many at all, try again using these different techniques:

Method 3: composite pictures

Imagining a composite picture can help you remember the words. Imagine a boat (*un barco*), 'put' an elephant (*un elefante*), eating an apple (*una manzana*), sitting on a chair (*una silla*) in the boat. 'Put' a tap (*un grifo*) on the front of the boat to let the water out. (5 words).

Introduction

Look through a window (*una ventana*) at a Christmas tree (*un á.... ...ue Navidad*), 'hang' a bicycle (*una bicicleta*), a flower (*una flor*) and a clock (*un reloj*) in the tree like Christmas decorations. Now put a light bulb (*una bombilla*) on the top. (6 words) What have you got left? Some gloves (*unos guantes*) – put them on to keep your hands warm.

Method 4: first letter groups

Grouping words by their first letter and first few letters can help you remember the words. Look again at the words in Method 1.
There are three which begin with **c: cab...; car...; cuch...**
There are three which begin with **p: p...; pl...;pu...**(you can eat two of them)
There are two which begin with **b: bo...; bu...**
There is one of each which begin with **a...; l...; t...; z...**
Now how many can you remember?

Which methods are best for me?

By which of these four methods do you remember best? Just one? Or a mixture of all of them?

Try again in five minutes ... and in half an hour ... and tomorrow.

Now you should know how you prefer to learn!

Learning AND remembering

It's one thing to remember words a short time after you have learned them. But will you remember them when you come across them again in the future? Stages **1-4** below revise the inital learning part of the process already described previously; stages **5** and beyond help you find 'pegs' in your mind on which to 'hang' the words you have learned, and so remember them better.

1 Below is a list of twelve words. Choose six of them to learn.

el aparcamiento	*car park*	la parada de autobús	*bus stop*
la autopista	*motorway*	el paso a nivel	*level crossing*
la carretera	*road*	el puente	*bridge*
el cruce	*crossroads*	el semáforo	*traffic lights*
la esquina	*corner*	la señal	*sign*
la estación	*station*	la zona peatonal	*pedestrian area*

Introduction

2 Put a **mark** beside the words you would like to learn.
Count them. (Choose six to try).
Underline the first letter of each word.

3 Read them aloud. (Put your hands over your ears whilst you do it). Try it again, until you are happy with the sound of them.

4 Now learn the words using the method or combination of methods (described previously) which suits you best.

5 Look at each word carefully for ways to remember it. Find 'pegs' to hang them on.

Does it sound like the English word*? (**estación** – *station*)
Does it sound like a different English word*? (**esquina** – sounds like *skin*)
Does part of it look like the English word*? (a{**parc**}amiento – *car park*)
* see the next section: *Tips for remembering*
Can you find any word that might be helpful? (**auto** – to do with cars)
Can you see a picture of each word, as you say it?
Can you picture it as it sounds? (**cruce** – *crossroads*)
Can you build all the words into an imaginary composite picture?
Say each word as you 'add' it to the picture.
(**carretera; cruce; semáforo;** ...)

6 Cover up the English and try to remember what your chosen words mean.

7 Write a list of the first letters and put dashes for the missing letters.
Which did you choose? **Mark** them ... and try to 'read' the words.

el a _ _ _ _ _ _ _ _ _ _ _	*car park* (parc/park)
la a _ _ _ _ _ _ _ _	*motorway* (auto)
la c _ _ _ _ _ _ _ _	*road* (car)
el c _ _ _ _	*crossroads* (first two letters same as English)
la e _ _ _ _ _ _	*corner* (sounds like skin)
la e _ _ _ _ _ _ _	*station* (sounds like the English word)
la p _ _ _ _ _ _ _ _ _ _ _ _ _ _ _	*bus stop* (bus)
el p _ _ _ _ _ _ _ _ _	*level crossing* (**nivel** sounds like level)
el p _ _ _ _ _	*bridge* (imagine punt going under bridge)

el s _ _ _ _ _ _ _ _	*traffic lights* (semaphore signals)
la s _ _ _ _	*sign* (sounds fairly similar)
la z _ _ _ _ _ _ _ _ _ _ _	*pedestrian area* (zone/area)

8 Fill in the missing letters and check that you have got them right.

9 Cover up the Spanish and see if you can remember the words you have chosen.

10 Do something else for half an hour.

11 Go back and check that you can still remember the six you chose.

car park	**el a** _ _ _ _ _ _ _ _ _ _ _
motorway	**la a** _ _ _ _ _ _ _ _
road	**la c** _ _ _ _ _ _ _ _
crossroads	**el c** _ _ _ _
corner	**la e** _ _ _ _ _ _
station	**la e** _ _ _ _ _ _ _
bus stop	**la p** _ _ _ _ _ _ _ _ _ _ _ _ _ _ _
level crossing	**el p** _ _ _ _ _ _ _ _
bridge	**el p** _ _ _ _ _
traffic lights	**el s** _ _ _ _ _ _ _
sign	**la s** _ _ _ _
pedestrian area	**la z** _ _ _ _ _ _ _ _ _ _ _

———— Tips for remembering ————

A good short cut to remembering is by linking Spanish to what you already know of English and/or other languages.

Words related to English

Does it sound like the English word or a related word?
The Spanish word for square is **plaza** – it sounds a bit like *place*
Does it look like the English word or a related word?
The Spanish word for garden is **jardín** – virtually the same word
The Spanish word for vegetable garden is **huerta** – as in *horticulture*

English is a particularly rich language with words from many sources. Some of the words we use come from a Northern origin, from

Introduction

the ancient Anglo-Saxon and Nordic languages and some from a Southern origin, from Latin, French and the Celtic languages as well as many words brought back by the early travellers from all round the globe.

Some examples of words used in English whose origin is in the Spanish language are:

chocolate	**chocolate**
potato	**patata**
guitar	**guitarra**
hammock	**hamaca**
cannibal	**canibal**
hurricane	**huracán**

English and Spanish share many words of Latin origin, which often makes learning new vocabulary easy. A few examples of words which are virtually the same (apart from pronunciation) are:

admiración	*admiration*
beneficio	*benefit*
calcular	*calculate*
dedicado	*dedicated*
formación	*formation*

Look for words that are similar to the English ones e.g. **Diario** is the Spanish word for 'newspaper'. It sounds like the English word 'diary'. **Día** means 'day' in Spanish, so **diario** really means 'daily'.

Repeated patterns between English and Spanish

Consonant/vowel changes

The English 'ph' is always **'f'** in Spanish

telephone	**teléfono**
photo	**foto**
graphic	**gráfico**

'-ed' at the end of an English word is often **'-ado'** or **'-ido'** in Spanish

reserved	**reservado**
included	**incluido**

Introduction

'-tion' at the end of an English word becomes '**-ción**' in Spanish
> *administration*   **administración**
> *relation*   **relación**

'ss' in English is often '**s**' in Spanish
> *permissive*   **permisivo**
> *possessive*   **posesivo**

'imm' in English becomes '**inm**' in Spanish
> *immediate*   **inmediato**
> *immense*   **inmenso**

'b' in English often changes to '**v**' in Spanish, and vice versa
> *automobile*   **automóvil**
> *have*   **haber**

's' at the beginning of a word becomes '**es**' in Spanish
> *school*   **escuela**
> *state*   **estado**

'th' at the beginning of a word in English is often just '**t**' in Spanish
> *theatre*   **teatro**
> *thermometer*   **termómetro**

English compound nouns

One characteristic of English is that two nouns can go together to form a compound noun, for example 'bread knife', 'shoulder bag', 'window frame' etc. In Spanish, the most common way of expressing these ideas is by reversing the nouns and adding '**de**' between them: 'credit card' therefore becomes '**tarjeta de crédito**' (literally 'card of credit'). Other examples are:

el billete de avión	*plane ticket*
el número de asiento	*seat number*
la tarjeta de embarque	*boarding card*
la salida de emergencia	*emergency exit*

Spanish adjectives as nouns

In Spanish, adjectives can also be used as nouns, whereas this is very rare in English. For example, 'the white ones' would be '**los blancos/las blancas**'; 'the red one' would be '**el rojo/la roja**'.

Introduction

Words related to other European languages

Look for words that are related to words you already know. A brief look at some of the other European languages may help you to recognise patterns that will help you to deduce the meaning of new words and help you to learn them more quickly.

English	German	French	Italian	Spanish	related English
father	Vater	père	padre	padre	paternity
flower	Blumen	fleur	flora	flor	bloom; floral
foot	Fuß	pied	piede	pie	pedal
grass	Gras	herbe	herba	hierba	herb
hunger	Hunger	faim	fame	hambre	famished
iron	Eisen	fer	ferro	hierro	ferrous (Fe)
man	Mann	homme	huomo	hombre	human
meat	Fleisch	viande	carne	carne	carnivorous; flesh
water	Wasser	eau	aqua	agua	aquarium

The English words in the column below are all of a 'Northern' origin, but each has related words from a 'Southern' origin which in many cases are very similar to the Spanish words. See if you can find the related words from the following list and add them to the right-hand column:

cavalry; chamber; corporation; corpse; dentist; habit; lunar; marine; mermaid; mural; nocturnal; robe; vest; terrestrial

English	French	Italian	Spanish	related English words
body	corps	corpo	cuerpo	
dress	robe	abito	vestido	
earth	terre	terra	tierra	
horse	cheval	cavallo	caballo	
moon	lune	luna	luna	
night	nuit	notte	noche	
room	chambre	camera	cámara	
sea	mer	mare	mar	
tooth	dent	dente	diente	
wall	mur	muro	muro	

Do you know any more related words which aren't in the list?

Introduction

Punctuation

Usage is the same in Spanish and English, but notice that inverted question and exclamation marks are placed at the beginning and end of the relevant sentence in Spanish.

¿Qué hora es?	*What's the time?*
¡Ten cuidado!	*Be careful!*
¡Socorro!	*Help!*

Notice too that at the beginning of a letter, a colon is used in Spanish, whereas a comma is preferred in English:

Querido José:	*Dear José,*

Focus and learn!

Most people make the excuse that they are no good at learning words as they have a poor memory. You don't! It is not your memory that is poor, it is failure to give it the guidance and focus it needs. In learning words from a list the learner has not yet decided when he or she is going to use them. There is no immediate goal.

To learn with least effort you need to have a set of clear goals. Choose your goals:

A I want to use the language to communicate with other speakers of that language:
  - on a business trip;
  - on a holiday trip;
  - on a social visit;
  - at home, for business reasons;
  - because I know someone I would like to talk to or write to.

B I want to be able to understand the language to:
  - read something in that language for pleasure, books, magazines, letters etc.;
  - read something for business, manuals, letters, faxes etc.;
  - listen to the radio;
  - watch television programmes;
  - read signs and instructions on a visit.

C I just enjoy learning languages.

You should choose the words and phrases, you are going to learn and focus on them and their meaning. Concentrating on the words and thinking about their meaning and the sound of them and looking for 'pegs' on which to 'hang' them (looking for related words, imaging them in pictures, remembering the sound of the words etc.) will help you to put them in your long term memory.

—— **List of abbreviations used** ——

(m.)	masculine noun
(f.)	feminine noun
(sing.)	singular form
(pl.)	plural form
(fam.)	familiar form of address
(form.)	formal/polite form of address

1 Saludos *Greetings*

Buenos días	*Good morning*	¿Qué tal?;	
Buenas tardes	*Good afternoon*	¿Qué hay?	*Hi!; How are you?*
Buenas tardes	*Good evening*	¿Cómo está?	
Buenas noches	*Good night* (greeting and taking leave)	(form.)	*How are you?*
		¿Cómo estás?	
		(fam.)	*How are you?*
Hola	*Hello*	Muy bien, gracias.	
Adiós	*Goodbye*	¿Y Usted?	*Very well, thank*
Hasta luego	*See you later*	(form.)	*you. And you?*
Hasta mañana	*See you tomorrow*	¿Y tú? (fam.)	*And you?*

¡OTRA VEZ!

● Activity: ¿Qué dirías? *What would you say?*

TRATAMIENTO
TITLES

formal titles used before first surname

Señor (Sr.)	*Mr; Sir*
Señora (Sra.)	*Mrs*
Señorita (Srta.)	*Miss*

Buenos días, Sr. López

formal titles used before first name

Don (D.)
Doña (Dña.)

Buenas tardes, Dña María

Usted (Vd.)	*you* (sing.)
Ustedes (Vds.)	*you* (pl.)

formal, polite forms of 'you'

2 Números *Numbers*

¡OTRA VEZ!

● *Activity:* ¿Qué dirías? *What would you say? (Look back to the previous page.)*

(a) Señor Suárez (b) Conchita (c) Doña María

NÚMEROS CARDINALES
CARDINAL NUMBERS

0	cero	20	veinte
1	uno (un), una	21	veintiuno (veintiún)
2	dos	22	veintidós
3	tres	30	treinta
4	cuatro	31	treinta y un(o)
5	cinco	40	cuarenta
6	seis	50	cincuenta
7	siete	60	sesenta
8	ocho	70	setenta
9	nueve	80	ochenta
10	diez	90	noventa
11	once	100	cien
12	doce	101	ciento uno
13	trece	500	quinientos (-as)
14	catorce	700	setecientos (-as)
15	quince	900	novecientos (-as)
16	dieciséis	1.000	mil
17	diecisiete	2.000	dos mil
18	dieciocho	1.000.000	un millón
19	diecinueve	2.000.000	dos millones

Notes on cardinal numbers

Numbers 1–30 are written as one word: 14: **catorce**; 22: **veintidós**.
Numbers 31–99 are written separately, with **y** between the tens and units:
33: **treinta y tres**; 67: **sesenta y siete**.
Y is not used, however, in numbers such as 101, 120, 1.067 etc.

2 Números *Numbers*

NÚMEROS ORDINALES
ORDINAL NUMBERS

primero-a	*first*
segundo-a	*second*
tercero-a	*third*
cuarto-a	*fourth*
quinto-a	*fifth*
sexto-a	*sixth*
séptimo-a	*seventh*
octavo-a	*eighth*
noveno-a	*ninth*
décimo-a	*tenth*

FRACCIONES
FRACTIONS

cuarto-a	*quarter*
medio-a	*half*
tres cuartos	*three quarters*
un kilo y medio	*a kilo and a half*
una vez	*once*
dos veces	*twice*
tres veces	*three times*

DECIMALES *DECIMALS*

A comma is used in Spanish instead of a point, and the numbers after the decimal are not said individually as in English:
8,92   ocho coma noventa y dos
10,75   diez coma setenta y cinco

¡OTRA VEZ!

● *Activity:* Practica y lee estos números de teléfonos y sus prefijos. *Practise reading these telephone numbers and codes.*

In Spain, numbers are said in pairs. 425788 would therefore be cuarenta y dos, cincuenta y siete, ochenta y ocho. 463 would be cuatro, sesenta y tres. 04 would be cero cuatro.

Try these:

93	217 62 92	(Barcelona)
91	732 80 44	(Madrid)
977	31 28 04	(Tarragona)
952	73 11 59	(Málaga)
945	15 99 01	(Vitoria)

What is your telephone number?

2 Números *Numbers*

In Spanish, years are read as complete numbers. A full stop and not a comma separates the thousands and hundreds. For example:
Nací en mil novecientos cincuenta y seis. (1.956)
I was born in nineteen fifty-six.

¡OTRA VEZ!

● *Activity:*

1 Read these years aloud:

1.975	1.984
1.998	2.025

Add important dates in your own life and practise saying them:

Nací en . . .	*I was born in . . .*
Empecé a trabajar en . . .	*I started work in . . .*
Me casé en . . .	*I got married in . . .*
Fui a la universidad en . . .	*I went to university in . . .*

2 The Big Race: Where did they come?

| Elena | Isabel | María |

20

3 El calendario *The calendar*

EL CALENDARIO
THE CALENDAR

el día	*day*
la semana	*week*
la quincena	*fortnight*
el mes	*month*
el año	*year*
el año bisiesto	*leap year*

LOS DÍAS DE LA SEMANA
THE DAYS OF THE WEEK

lunes	*Monday*
martes	*Tuesday*
miércoles	*Wednesday*
jueves	*Thursday*
viernes	*Friday*
sábado	*Saturday*
domingo	*Sunday*
la mañana	*morning*
el mediodía	*midday*
la tarde	*afternoon; evening*
la noche	*night*
hoy	*today*
mañana	*tomorrow*
pasado mañana	*the day after tomorrow*
ayer	*yesterday*
anteayer	*the day before yesterday*
esta mañana	*this morning*
ayer por la tarde	*yesterday afternoon*
mañana por la tarde	*tomorrow evening*
el fin de semana	*the weekend*

LOS MESES
THE MONTHS

enero	*January*
febrero	*February*
marzo	*March*
abril	*April*
mayo	*May*
junio	*June*
julio	*July*
agosto	*August*
septiembre	*September*
octubre	*October*
noviembre	*November*
diciembre	*December*

In Spanish, the days of the week and months do not start with a capital letter.

DATES

Cardinal numbers (dos, tres, cuatro, etc.) are used for dates in Spanish, except for the first of each month (el primero).

el primero de enero	*1st January*
el dos de febrero	*2nd February*
el tres de marzo	*3rd March*
el veinte de abril	*20th April*

No preposition is used before the date:

Llegué el diez de noviembre.	*I arrived on the tenth of November.*

LAS CUATRO ESTACIONES
THE FOUR SEASONS

(en) invierno	*(in) winter*
(en) primavera	*(in) spring*
(en) verano	*(in) summer*
(en) otoño	*(in) autumn*

The seasons are masculine, except la primavera.

FIESTAS
HOLIDAYS

la Navidad	*Christmas*
la Semana Santa	*Easter / Holy Week*

3 El calendario *The calendar*

La Navidad

Christmas Eve (**Nochebuena**) is a more important day than Christmas Day in Spain. **Turrón** (*nougat*), **mazapán** (*marzipan cakes*) and **polvorones** (*shortbread cakes*) are traditional delicacies served at the end of the evening meal. Houses are decorated with a model crib (**Belén**) and sometimes with a Christmas tree. 'Merry Christmas' in Spanish is **Felices Navidades**. Children traditionally receive their presents from the Three Kings on January 6.

La Semana Santa

Holy Week is an important celebration throughout Spain. Statues of saints, virgins or scenes from the crucifixion are carried through the streets on floats (**pasos**), lit by candles and usually accompanied by music. The processions in Sevilla and Valladolid are particularly famous.

Días de Fiesta *National Public Holidays*

1° de enero	Día de Año Nuevo	New Year's Day
6 de enero	Día de los Reyes Magos	Epiphany
1° de mayo	Fiesta del Trabajo	Labour Day
25 de julio	Día de Santiago	St James' Day (Patron Saint of Spain)
12 de octubre	Día de la Hispanidad	Columbus Day
1° de noviembre	Todos los Santos	All Saint's Day
6 de diciembre	Día de la Constitución	Constitution Day

In addition to these national holidays, Spain has various holidays particular to individual regions.

Las Fallas take place on March 19 in Valencia. Models satirising political and other public figures are ceremonially burnt in the main squares.

La Feria de Abril is an annual event in Sevilla. It is a week-long celebration of flamenco costumes and dancing, horse riding and sherry.

San Fermín is a fiesta held in Pamplona from the 6th to the 15th of July. It is especially famous for the **encierros**, when bulls run free through the streets and locals and tourists test their courage by running in front of them.

¡OTRA VEZ!

● *Activity:*

1 ¿Cuándo son los cumpleaños?
(cumpleaños   =

¿Cuándo es tu (fam.)/su (form.)
cumpleaños?

Mi cumpleaños es el . . .
El cumpleaños de mi madre/
padre es el . . .
El cumpleaños de mi hija/
hijo es el . . .

2 ¿Cuándo son las reuniones?

Say when the birthdays are:
birthday)

When is your birthday?

My birthday is . . .
My mother's/father's birthday
is . . .
My daughter's/son's
birthday is . . .

When are the meetings?

(a) 10 JAN (b) 16 MAR (c) 22 JUN (d) 1 OCT (e) 15 NOV

¿Cuántos días hay en una semana?	*How many days are there in a week?*
¿Cuántas semanas hay en un mes?	*How many weeks are there in a month?*
¿Cuántos meses hay en un año?	*How many months are there in a year?*

4 El reloj *The clock*

¿QUÉ HORA ES?
WHAT TIME IS IT?

Es . . .	*It is . . .*
la una en punto	*one o'clock*
la una y cinco	*five past one*
la una y media	*half past one*
Son . . .	*It is . . .*
las dos y diez	*ten past two*

las dos y cuarto	*quarter past two*
las dos y veinte	*twenty past two*
las dos y media	*half past two*
las tres menos cuarto	*quarter to three*
la tres menos diez	*ten to three*
las tres en punto	*three o'clock*

La hora digital

las trece cero siete	13.07
las quince diecinueve	15.19
las diecinueve cincuenta y cuatro	19.54
las veintidós cuarenta y siete	22.47

la mañana	*morning*
la tarde	*afternoon; early evening*
la noche	*night*
¿Tiene hora? (form.)	*Have you got the time?*
¿Tienes hora? (fam.)	*Have you got the time?*
¿A qué hora?	*At what time?*

a las diez en punto de la mañana	*at ten o'clock in the morning*
a las cinco de la tarde	*at five o'clock in the afternoon*
el mediodía	*midday*
la medianoche	*midnight*
el reloj	*clock; watch*
la correa del reloj	*watchstrap*

Mi reloj adelanta/atrasa.	*My watch is fast / slow.*
Lo siento, llego tarde.	*Sorry I'm late.*
Mi reloj no funciona/está roto.	*My watch doesn't work / is broken.*
He perdido mi reloj.	*I have lost my watch.*
Necesito una pila nueva para mi reloj.	*I need a new battery for my watch.*

4 El reloj *The clock*

'am' is expressed by **de la mañana**.

son las diez de la mañana   *It's 10am.*

'pm' is expressed by **de la tarde** for the afternoon and evening and by **de la noche** for later hours:

Son las cinco de la tarde.   *It's 5pm.*
Son las once y media de la noche.   *It's 11.30pm.*

por la mañana   *in the morning*
por la tarde   *in the afternoon / early evening*
por la noche   *at night*

If no specific time is mentioned, one of the above may be used.

¡OTRA VEZ!

● *Activity:* Dí a qué hora es la cita. *Practise saying these times:*

¿A qué hora quedamos?   *When shall we meet?*
¿Qué tal a la/las . . .?   *What about at . . .?*

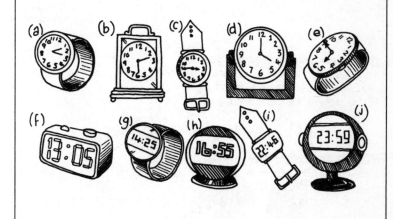

5 Los colores *Colours*

amarillo-a	*yellow*	rojo-a	*red*
azul	*blue*	rosa	*pink*
azul celeste	*light blue*	turquesa	*turquoise*
azul marino	*navy blue*	verde	*green*
beige	*beige*	violeta	*violet*
blanco-a	*white*		
dorado-a	*gold(en)*	oscuro	*dark*
gris	*grey*	claro	*light; pale*
marrón	*brown*	vivo	*bright*
morado-a	*purple*	fluorescente	*fluorescent*
naranja	*orange*		
negro-a	*black*	verde claro	*light green*
plateado-a	*silver*	verde oscuro	*dark green*

Colours are adjectives and must therefore agree in number and, if they end in **-o**, in gender with the noun they qualify: e.g. **la** camisa blan**ca**; **el** coche negr**o**; **los** ojos azul**es**.

Note that some colours have the same form for masculine and feminine nouns: e.g. **el** gato **gris**; **la** camisa **gris**.

¡OTRA VEZ!

● *Activity:*

1 ¿De qué color quieres que sean?
  What colours would you like them to be?
  Describe los jerseys y los pantalones.
  Describe the jerseys and trousers.

2 ¿De qué color son los banderas?
  What colours are the flags of the following countries?
  USA; UK; Italy; France; Germany; Spain

6 Adjetivos *Adjectives*

abierto-a	*open*	doble	*double*
aburrido-a	*boring; bored*	domesticado-a	*tame*
activo-a	*active*	dulce	*soft; sweet*
afectuoso-a	*warm*	duro-a	*hard; difficult*
afilado-a	*sharp*	educado-a	*polite*
alto-a	*tall; high*	en forma	*fit*
alto-a	*loud*	enfermo-a	*ill*
amable	*friendly*	equivocado-a	*wrong*
amargo-a	*bitter*	estrecho-a	*narrow*
ancho-a	*wide*	estúpido-a	*stupid*
animado-a	*lively*	extenso-a	*wide*
antiguo-a	*old; ancient*	fácil	*easy*
antipático-a	*unfriendly*	falso-a	*false*
áspero-a	*rough*	famoso-a	*famous*
bajo-a	*low; short*	feo-a	*ugly*
barato-a	*cheap*	frágil	*fragile*
bien	*well*	fresco-a	*fresh; cool*
blando-a	*soft*	frío-a	*cold*
bonito-a	*nice*	fuerte	*strong*
bueno-a	*good*	generoso-a	*generous*
caliente	*hot; warm*	gordo-a	*fat*
cansado-a	*tired*	grande	*big*
caro-a	*expensive*	gratis	*free (no cost)*
cercano-a	*nearby; near*	grosero-a	*rude*
ciego-a	*blind*	guapo	*handsome*
claro-a	*clear; light*	holgazán-ana	*idle*
cobarde	*cowardly*	horrible	*horrible*
cojo-a	*lame*	imposible	*impossible*
complicado-a	*complicated*	ingenioso-a	*clever*
contento-a	*happy*	inocente	*innocent*
correcto-a	*right; correct*	inteligente	*intelligent*
corriente	*common*	interesante	*interesting*
culpable	*guilty*	joven	*young*
débil	*weak*	justo-a	*fair (decision)*
delgado-a	*thin*	largo-a	*long*
divertido-a	*fun*	lejano-a	*far*

6 Adjetivos *Adjectives*

lento-a	*slow*	profundo-a	*deep*
libre	*free (not occupied)*	querido-a	*dear (beloved)*
limpio-a	*clean*	rápido-a	*quick*
lindo-a	*pretty*	raro-a	*strange; rare*
listo-a	*ready*	salvaje	*wild*
lleno-a	*full*	seco-a	*dry*
malo-a	*bad*	sencillo-a	*easy; single*
minusválido-a	*handicapped*		*(ticket, room)*
moderno-a	*modern*	simpático-a	*friendly*
mojado-a	*wet*	sordo-a	*deaf*
muerto-a	*dead*	suave	*soft*
nuevo-a	*new*	sucio-a	*dirty*
ocupado-a	*busy*	tacaño-a	*mean*
ocupado-a	*occupied (engaged)*	tarde	*late*
oscuro-a	*dark*	templado-a	*warm*
pasado-a	*last (last week)*	temprano-a	*early*
pasivo-a	*passive*	terrible	*terrible*
pequeño-a	*small*	tierno-a	*tender*
perezoso-a	*lazy*	tranquilo-a	*quiet; calm*
pesado-a	*heavy; boring*	triste	*sad*
plano-a	*flat*	último-a	*last; latest*
poco amable	*unfriendly*	vacío-a	*empty*
poco profundo-a	*shallow*	valiente	*brave*
posible	*possible*	verdadero-a	*true*
precioso-a	*beautiful*	viejo-a	*old*
primero-a	*first*	vivo-a	*alive*

¡OTRA VEZ!

● Activity: *Choose any twelve words from the list and write them down here, and then write down their opposites beside them.*

bueno - malo   *good - bad*

_____   _____

_____   _____

_____   _____

_____   _____

_____   _____

_____   _____

7 Adverbios *Adverbs*

ADVERBS

You can use these words to modify what you are saying about something.

Ella es **bastante** alta. *She is **quite** tall.*
El **siempre** llega tarde. *He is **always** late.*

ahora	*now, just now*	mal	*badly*
antes	*before*	más	*more*
alto	*loudly*	menos	*less*
bajo	*softly*	mucho	*much; many*
bastante	*rather*	muy	*very*
bastante;		poco	*little; few*
suficiente	*enough*	por lo menos	*at least*
bien	*well*	por término	
casi	*almost*	medio	*on average*
claramente	*clearly*	precisamente	*exactly, precisely*
completamente	*completely*	probablemente	*probably*
demasiado	*too (much; many)*	quizá	*perhaps*
desgraciadamente	*unfortunately*	realmente	*really*
especialmente	*specially*	solamente	*only*
exactamente	*exactly*	también	*also*
lentamente	*slowly*	totalmente	*completely*

¡OTRA VEZ!

● Activity: *Modify these sentences by adding a word in the gaps:*

Marta es _____ alta.	Marta is _____ tall.
Estoy _____ cansado.	I am _____ tired.
Mis hermanas cantan _____ .	My sisters sing _____ .
Hace _____ calor.	It is _____ hot.
Tengo _____ dinero.	I've got _____ money.

8 ¿Dónde? *Where?*

a	*to*	en casa	*at home*
a la izquierda	*on the left*	en el centro (de)	*in the middle of*
a la derecha	*on the right*	en lo alto (de)	*at the top of*
a través (de)	*through*	en ninguna parte	*nowhere*
abajo	*down*	en todas partes	*everywhere*
adelante	*forward*	encima (de)	*above*
ahí	*there*	enfrente (de)	*opposite*
al fondo (de)	*at the end of*	entre	*between*
alrededor (de)	*around*	fuera (de)	*outside*
aquí	*here*	hacia	*towards*
arriba	*up*	junto a	*beside*
cerca (de)	*near*	lejos (de)	*far from*
debajo (de)	*under*	más allá (de)	*beyond*
delante (de)	*in front of*	por delante	*past*
dentro (de)	*in*	por encima (de)	*over*
detrás (de)	*behind*	posterior,	
en	*in, at, on*	de atrás	*back*
en alguna parte	*somewhere*	sobre	*on*

¡OTRA VEZ!

● Activity: ¿Dónde está Alberto? *Where's Alberto?*

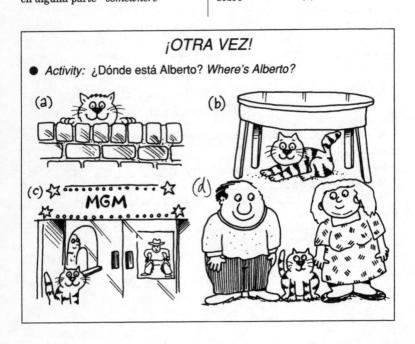

30

9 ¿Cuándo? *When?*

actualmente	*nowadays*	luego	*next*
alguna vez,		mañana	*tomorrow*
a veces	*sometimes*	más tarde	*afterwards, later*
antes de	*before*	mientras	*while*
aún (más)	*still (more)*	nunca	*never*
ayer	*yesterday*	otra vez	*again*
con frecuencia,		por lo general	*usually*
a menudo	*often*	primero	*first*
de vez en cuando	*from time to time*	pronto	*soon*
después	*after*	recientemente	*recently*
el año pasado	*last year*	siempre	*always*
entonces	*then*	tan pronto como	*as soon as*
entre tanto	*meanwhile*	tarde	*late*
este año	*this year*	temprano	*early*
finalmente	*finally*	todavía	*still*
hace	*ago*	último-a	*last*
hasta	*until*	una vez	*once*
hoy	*today*	ya	*already*
inmediatamente	*immediately*		

¡OTRA VEZ!

● Activity: *Add a word to complete these sentences and their translations:*

1) Vamos _____ a España de vacaciones.
   We _____ go to Spain for our holidays.

2) Vamos a ir _____ al centro.
   _____ we are going to the centre.

3) _____ fuimos a otro restaurante.
   _____ we went to another restaurant.

4) _____ hace buen tiempo pero _____ llueve.
   _____ the weather is good but _____ it rains.

---

10 Pronombres interrogativos *Question words*

¿Cómo? — *How?*
¿Cómo estás? — *How are you?*

¿Cuándo? — *When?*
¿Cuándo es la fiesta? — *When is the party?*

¿Cuánto? — *How much?*
¿Cuánto dinero tienes? — *How much money have you got?*

¿Cuántos-as? — *How many?*
¿Cuántos coches tienen? — *How many cars have they got?*

¿Cuál? — *Which?*
¿Cuál te gusta? — *Which one do you like?*

¿Dónde? — *Where?*
¿Dónde quedamos? — *Where shall we meet?*

¿De dónde? — *Where from?*
¿De dónde eres? — *Where are you from?*

¿A dónde? — *Where to?*
¿A dónde vamos? — *Where shall we go?*

¿Por qué? — *Why?*
¿Por qué llegas tarde? — *Why are you late?*

¿Qué? — *What?*
¿Qué es esto? — *What is this?*

¿Quién? — *Who?*
¿Quién eres? — *Who are you?*

¿Qué clase de . . . ? — *What kind of . . . ?*
¿Qué clase de música te gusta? — *What kind of music do you like?*

¡OTRA VEZ!

● *Activity: What was the question?*

Por ejemplo:
Respuesta: *Answer:*
Son las dos y media.   *It's half past two.*
Pregunta: *Question:*
¿Qué hora es?   *What time is it?*

Preguntas:	Respuestas:
1 ¿_____?	2.000 pesetas
2 ¿_____?	Sr. Álvarez.
3 ¿_____?	Un Citroën
4 ¿_____?	En el jardín.
5 ¿_____?	Bien, gracias.

11 Artículos, adjetivos demostrativos y posesivos, pronombres y conjunciones
Articles, demonstrative and possessive adjectives, pronouns and conjunctions

---

Artículo determinado   The definite article

el; la; los; las	the

Artículo indeterminado   The indefinite article

un; una	a	unos, unas	some

Adjetivos demostrativos   Demonstrative adjectives

este; esta	this	estos; estas	these
eso; esa	that	esos; esas	those

Adjetivos posesivos   Possessive adjectives

mi (s)	my	mío-a (s)	mine
tu (s)	your	tuyo-a (s)	yours (fam.)
su (s)	his, her, its, your (form.)	suyo-a (s)	his, her, its, yours (form.)
nuestro-a (s)	our	nuestro-a (s)	ours
vuestro-a (s)	your	vuestro-a (s)	yours
sus	their	suyo-a (s)	theirs, yours (form. pl)

The forms mío/a, tuyo/a etc., can follow a noun:

un amigo mío	a (male) friend of mine
una colega mía	a (female) colleague of mine

or if used after a verb, the definite article is placed in front:

esta oficina es la mía	this office is mine
este billete es el tuyo	this ticket is yours

Pronombres sujeto   Subject pronouns

yo	I	nosotros-as	we
tú	you (fam.)	vosotros-as	you (fam. pl.)
usted	you (form.)	ustedes	you (form. pl.)
él	he	ellos-as	they
ella	she		

(Refer to Section 1 – Greetings and Titles, page 17.)

In Spanish, the subject pronouns are not often used for verbs whose endings show who or what the subject is. For example, it is not necessary to say **Yo soy de Londres** (*I am from London*) but simply **Soy de Londres**, as **soy** can only refer to *I*.

Use **tú** when addressing children, friends, young people, relatives or when invited to do so. Otherwise, use **usted**.

Preposition forms:

menos yo	except me	para tí	for you
de tu parte	from you	para él	for him
para mí	for me	para ella	for her

---

para nosotros-as	*for us*	consigo	*with him / herself*
		con él	*with him*
conmigo	*with me*	sin ellos-as	*without them*
contigo	*with you* (fam.)		

Pronombres complemento *Object pronouns*

These can be direct (**Lo** haré – *I'll do it*) or indirect (¿Qué **me** recomienda? – *What do you recommend to me?*)

me	*me / to me*	nos	*us / to us*
te	*you / to you* (fam.)	os	*you / to you* (fam. pl.)
le	*you / to you* (form.)	les	*you / to you*
	him / to him		(form. pl.)
la	*her / to her*		*them / to them*
	it / to it (fem.)	las	*them / to them* (fem.)
lo	*him / to him*	los	*them / to them* (masc.)

Conjunciones *Conjunctions*

aunque	*although*	o	*or*
cuando	*when*	si	*if*
pero	*but*	y	*and*
porque	*because*		

¿**Me** llama a las siete?	*Will you call me at 7?*
¿**Me** trae la cuenta?	*Could you bring me the bill?*
¿**Me** dice la hora?	*Could you tell me the time?*
¿Puede ayudar**me**?	*Could you help me?*
Necesito **un** plano de Madrid	*I need a street plan of Madrid*
¿Dónde está **la** salida?	*Where is the exit?*
Él es inglés	*He is English*
Lo/la compro	*I'll buy it*
Este es **mi** pasaporte	*This is my passport*
¿Dónde está **el tuyo**?	*Where's yours?*
María es una amiga **mía**	*Maria is a friend of mine*
Nos gusta viajar **pero** ...	*We like travelling but ...*
Nos da miedo el avión	*We're afraid of flying*
Para mí, ensalada **y** pollo	*For me, salad and chicken*

¡OTRA VEZ!

● *Activity: Put the right form of:* **1** this/these **2** my **3** our

in front of these words:

libro; libros; casa; casas; coche; familia; restaurante

12 Verbos *Verbs*

There are three categories of Spanish verbs, according to the ending of the infinitive: either **-ar**, **-er** or **-ir** (**hablar** – *to speak*, **comer** – *to eat*, **vivir** – *to live*). Some verbs are regular, which means they follow a set pattern, whereas others are irregular, as they deviate from this pattern in places. This deviation usually takes the form of a vowel change in the middle of the word, or occasionally the first person singular in the present tense has a distinct form (e.g.: **doy**, **digo**, **hago**– *I give, I say, I do*).

In some respects Spanish verbs are more complicated than English verbs, as there is a separate form for each person and for the singular and plural. However, in Spanish there is no equivalent of 'do/does' or 'did'; negatives are formed simply by adding **no** before the verbs e.g.

No fumo.	*I don't smoke.*

and verbs in questions have the same form as the affirmative, e.g.

¿Dónde vives?	*Where do you live?*

In compound tenses, the auxiliary verb **haber** is used together with the past participle:

Este verano he viajado por el Norte de España.	*This summer I travelled around the north of Spain.*
¿Has visto mi libro?	*Have you seen my book?*

For more about verb formation and endings, see *Teach Yourself Spanish Verbs.*

MAIN VERB TENSES

Presente
Viajo mucho.

Present
I travel a lot.

Pretérito indefinido
Viajé a España en 1992.

Past
I went to Spain in 1992.

Pretérito perfecto.
He viajado mucho.

Perfect
I have travelled a lot.

Pretérito imperfecto
Antes viajaba mucho.

Imperfect
I used to travel a lot.

Futuro
Viajaré a Asturias en mayo.

The future
I'll go to Asturias in May.

12 Verbos *Verbs*

SER *AND* ESTAR
TO BE

The verb 'to be' is expressed in Spanish either by **ser** or **estar**. These verbs are not interchangeable and both are irregular.

Ser

Ser is used in the following situations:

Name	Soy María López.	*I am María Lopez.*
Nationality	Soy inglés.	*I am English.*
Origin	Es de Londres.	*He / she / it is from London.*
Occupation	Soy médico.	*I am a doctor.*
Possession	Es mi coche.	*It's my car.*
Time	¿Qué hora es?	*What time is it?*
Date	Hoy es el 10 de agosto.	*Today is the 10th of August.*
	Es martes.	*It's Tuesday.*
Price	¿Cuánto es?	*How much is it?*
	Son 1000 pesetas.	*It's 1000 pesetas.*
Quantity	Es suficiente/mucho.	*It's enough / a lot.*
Size	Es pequeño-a/grande.	*It's small / big.*
Height	Es bajo-a/alto-a.	*It's short / tall.*

Ser is also used when talking about political or religious persuasion.

Estar

Estar is used with a preposition or adverb to indicate:

Location	Estoy en el bar.	*I'm in the bar.*
Position	Está cerca.	*It's near.*

It is also used for moods, well-being and state of health:

¿Cómo estás?	*How are you?*
Estoy bien, gracias.	*I'm fine, thanks.*

With an adjective, **estar** also expresses a temporary state or quality:

Está libre.	*It's free.*
Está cerrado hoy.	*It's closed today.*
Está completo.	*It's full.*

TENER *TO HAVE*

Tener is used to express age:

¿Cuántos años tienes?	*How old are you?*
Tengo doce años.	*I am 12.*

To talk about your family:

Tengo dos hermanas.	*I've got two sisters.*
¿Tienes hijos?	*Have you got any children?*

To talk about your possessions:

Tengo un coche viejo.	*I've got an old car.*

It is also used in several idiomatic expressions:

Tengo . . .	*I'm . . .*
frío	*cold*
calor	*hot*
hambre	*hungry*
sed	*thirsty*
miedo	*afraid*
sueño	*sleepy*
prisa	*in a hurry*
razón	*right*

Other expressions which use **tener** are:

¿Tiene hora?	*Have you got the time?*
Aquí tiene.	*Here you are.*
Tengo una habitación reservada.	*I have a room reserved.*

Note that **tener que + infinitive** expresses the idea of obligation:

Tengo que llamar por teléfono.	*I have to make a phone call.*

IR *TO GO*

¿Adónde vas?	*Where are you going?*
Voy a la playa	*I'm going to the beach*

Ir + a + infinitive is used to express the immediate future:

¿Qué vas a hacer este verano?	*What are you going to do this summer?*

Voy a ir a Francia.	*I'm going to France.*
Voy a visitar a mi hermano.	*I'm going to visit my brother.*

HAY *THERE IS/ARE*

¿Dónde hay una parada de taxis?	*Where is there a taxi rank?*
Hay dos supermercados	*There are two supermarkets*
¿Hay una mesa libre?	*Is there a free table?*
¿Hay una plaza en este tren?	*Is there a seat on this train?*

Hay is used in the greeting:

¡Hola, Pedro! ¿Qué hay?	*Hello Pedro. How're things?*

Hay can also be used to express obligation or necessity:

Hay que tomar el sol con precaución.	*You must be careful when you're sunbathing.*
Hay que estar en el aeropuerto una hora antes del vuelo.	*You must be at the airport an hour before the flight.*

USEFUL VERB COMBINATIONS

The following expressions can be combined with the infinitive of both regular and irregular verbs (without an additional preposition):

Quisiera/quisiéramos . . .	*I / we would like . . .*
Quisiera alquilar un coche.	*I would like to rent a car.*
Voy/vamos a . . .	*I / we are going to . . .*
Vamos a llegar a las cinco.	*We'll be arriving at 5.*
Me/nos gustaría . . .	*I / we would like (to) . . .*
Me gustaría tomar café.	*I'd like to have a coffee.*
Tengo/tenemos que . . .	*I / we have to . . .*
Tengo que trabajar mañana.	*I've got to work tomorrow.*
Prefiero/preferimos . . .	*I / we prefer . . .*
Prefiero el vino tinto.	*I prefer red wine.*
Debo/debemos . . .	*I / we must / ought to . . .*
Debemos salir pronto.	*We must leave early.*
Espero/esperamos . . .	*I / we hope to . . .*
Espero terminar el informe pronto.	*I hope to finish the report soon.*

Hay que ...   *You must / it is necessary to ...*
Hay que comprobar el aceite.   *It's necessary to check the oil.*

¿Se puede ...?   *Is it possible to ...?*
¿Se puede aparcar aquí?   *Is it possible to park here?*

EL ASPECTO PERSONAL
PERSONAL APPEARANCE

Soy . . .	*I am . . .*
El/Ella es . . .	*He / she is . . .*
alto-a	*tall*
bajo-a	*short*
de estatura mediana	*medium height*
delgado-a	*thin*
fuerte	*well built*
gordo-a	*fat*

Tengo el pelo . . .	*I have . . . hair*
blanco	*white*
caoba	*auburn*
castaño	*chestnut*
claro	*fair*
corto	*short*
gris	*grey*
lacio	*straight*
largo	*long*
ondulado	*wavy*
oscuro	*dark*
pelirrojo	*red*
rizado	*curly*
rubio	*blond*

y los ojos . . .	*and . . . eyes*
azules	*blue*
azul-grises	*blue-grey*
marrones	*brown*
negros	*black*
verdes	*green*

Soy miope/hipermétrope.	*I am short / long sighted.*
Llevo gafas	*I wear glasses*
Llevo lentillas	*I wear contact lenses*

Soy . . .	*I am . . .*
bien parecido-a	*good looking*
guapo-a	*handsome*

1 **Asuntos personales** *Personal matters*

el peso	*weight*
Peso . . . kgs.	*I weigh . . . kgs.*
Soy de piel . . .	*I am . . . skinned*
blanca	*fair*
morena	*dark*
pálida	*pale*
Estoy bronceado-a.	*I'm suntanned.*
El/ella tiene . . .	*He/she has . . .*
acné	*acne*
arrugas	*wrinkles*
barba	*a beard*
bigote	*a moustache*
la boca ancha	*a wide mouth*
la boca pequeña	*a narrow mouth*
una bonita sonrisa	*a nice smile*
las cejas pobladas	*bushy eyebrows*
una cicatriz	*a scar*
la curva de la felicidad	*a beer belly*
un grano/granos	*a spot/spots*
la frente despejada	*a high forehead*
hoyüelos	*dimples*
los labios carnosos/finos	*thick/thin lips*
un lunar	*a mole*
una mancha de nacimiento	*a birth mark*
las orejas grandes/pequeñas	*big/small ears*
pecas	*freckles*
la nariz aguileña	*a Roman nose*
chata	*a button nose*
de boxeador	*a boxer's nose*
grande	*a big nose*
respingona	*an upturned nose*
torcida	*broken nose*
Está calvo.	*He is bald.*
El/ella es . . .	*He/she is . . .*
feo-a	*ugly*
guapo-a	*handsome, beautiful*
mono-a/lindo-a	*sweet/cute*

1 Asuntos personales *Personal matters*

El/ella está . . .	*He/she is . . .*
bien arreglado-a	*well groomed*
desaliñado-a	*scruffy*
limpio-a	*clean*
sucio-a	*dirty*

| ¡Qué guapa! | *She's really beautiful.* |
| ¡El no está nada mal tampoco! | *He's not bad either!* |

¡OTRA VEZ!

● *Activity:* ¿Cómo eres? *What are you like?*

Estoy _____ I am _____

_____ _____

Soy _____ I am _____

_____ _____

Tengo _____ I have _____

_____ _____

1 Asuntos personales *Personal matters*

EL CURRICULUM VITAE

Mi Curriculum Vitae *My CV*

Nombre	*First Name*
Apellido	*Surname*
Edad	*Age*
Estado civil	*Married / single*
Fecha de nacimiento	*Date of birth*
Lugar de nacimiento	*Place of birth*
Nacionalidad	*Nationality*
Estudios	*Education*
Experiencia	*Experience*
Aficiones	*Interests*

SENTIMIENTOS Y EMOCIONES
FEELINGS AND EMOTIONS

la alegría	*happiness; joy*
la compasión	*compassion*
el descontento	*dissatisfaction*
la emoción	*emotion*
el entusiasmo	*enthusiasm*
el (buen/mal) humor	*(good / bad) mood*
el miedo	*fear*
la satisfacción	*satisfaction*
el sentimiento	*feeling*
la simpatía	*sympathy*
el terror	*dread*
la tristeza	*sadness*

Estoy . . .	*I am / feel . . .*
aburrido-a	*bored*
agotado-a	*drained*
alegre	*happy*
apenado-a	*distressed*
asqueado-a	*disgusted*
avergonzado-a	*ashamed*
cansado-a	*tired*
contentísimo-a	*overjoyed*
contento-a	*happy*
deprimido-a	*depressed*
descontento-a	*dissatisfied*
encantado-a	*delighted*
enfermo-a/bien	*ill / well*
en forma	*fit*
hablador-a	*talkative*
hecho polvo	*shattered; exhausted*
horrorizado-a	*appalled*
inquieto-a	*apprehensive*

mejor/peor	*better / worse*
molesto-a	*annoyed*
preocupado-a	*concerned; worried*
rendido-a	*exhausted*
sorprendido-a	*surprised*
triste	*sad*

Me siento . . .   *I am / feel . . .*

animado-a	*lively*
defraudado-a	*let down*
de maravilla	*great!*
emocionado-a	*emotional*
entusiasta	*enthusiastic*
fabuloso-a	*terrific*
fatal	*terrible*
optimista	*hopeful*
rechazado-a	*rejected*
relajado-a	*relaxed; laid back*
sexy	*sexy*
violento-a	*violent*

Tengo . . .   *I am / feel . . .*

alegría	*happy*
curiosidad	*curious*
envidia	*envy*
hambre	*hungry*
miedo	*frightened*
sed	*thirsty*
sueño	*sleepy*
temor	*afraid*

¿Cómo te encuentras?	*How are you feeling?*
Estoy de buen/mal humor.	*I am in a good / bad mood.*

El/ella está . . .   *He / she is . . .*

sonriendo	*smiling*
llorando	*crying*

CARACTERÍSTICAS
CHARACTERISTICS

¿Qué clase de persona eres?	*What sort of a person are you?*

Soy . . .	*I am . . .*
abierto-a; franco-a	*open; frank*
aburrido-a	*boring*
afable	*pleasant*
alegre	*cheerful*
amable	*gentle; friendly*
ambicioso-a	*ambitious*
antipático-a	*nasty; unfriendly*
arrogante	*arrogant*
astuto-a	*cunning*
atento-a	*considerate*
avaricioso-a	*greedy*
callado-a	*quiet*
cariñoso-a	*affectionate*
celoso-a	*jealous*
compasivo-a	*sympathetic*
confiado-a	*confident*
cruel	*cruel*
curioso-a	*curious*
de confianza	*trustworthy*
despistado-a	*absent minded*
despótico-a	*overbearing*
diestro-a/ zurdo-a	*right-handed / left-handed*
diplomático-a	*tactful*
divertido-a	*humorous; fun*
educado-a	*polite*
egoísta	*selfish*
encantador-a	*charming*
envidioso-a	*envious*
estúpido-a	*stupid*
feliz	*happy*
formal	*well behaved*
generoso-a	*generous*
gracioso-a	*funny*
grosero-a	*rude*

honorado-a	*honest*
impaciente	*impatient*
inculto-a	*rough*
ingenuo-a	*naive*
inocente	*innocent*
insolente	*insolent*
inteligente	*intelligent*
irresponsable	*irresponsible*
juicioso-a	*wise*
modesto-a	*modest*
nervioso-a	*nervous*
obstinado-a	*obstinate*
ordinario-a	*coarse; vulgar*
orgulloso-a	*proud*
paciente	*patient*
perezoso-a	*lazy*
precavido-a	*cautious*
presumido-a	*boastful*
prudente	*prudent*
raro-a	*strange*
razonable	*reasonable*
refinado-a	*refined*
rencoroso-a	*spiteful*
reservado-a	*reserved*
respetable	*respectable*
reticente	*reticent*
sagaz	*shrewd*
sensible	*sensitive*
serio-a	*serious*
servicial	*helpful*
sigiloso-a	*secretive*
simpático-a	*friendly*
sincero-a	*sincere*
tacaño-a	*miserly*
tímido-a	*timid*
tolerante	*tolerant*
torpe	*clumsy; dim witted*
trabajador-a	*hard-working*
travieso-a	*mischievous*
valeroso-a	*courageous*
valiente	*brave*
vengativo-a	*vindictive*
violento-a	*violent*

1 **Asuntos personales** *Personal matters*

GUSTOS Y PREFERENCIAS
LIKES AND DISLIKES

Me gusta-n	*I like*
No me gusta-n	*I don't like*
Me gustaría	*I would like*
Prefiero	*I prefer*
Me encanta-n	*I love*

aborrecer	*to abhor*
admirar	*to admire*
adorar	*to adore*
despreciar	*to despise*
odiar	*to hate*
ser aficionado-a a	*to be fond of*
ser entusiasta de	*to be a fan of*

Note the structure of the verbs **gustar** and **encantar**.

Me gusta el vino.	*I like wine.*
	(lit. *Wine is pleasing to me.*)
Me gustan los gatos.	*I like cats.*
Similarly:	
Me encanta la música.	*I love music.*

To form the negative, **no** is placed at the beginning of the sentence:

No me gusta el café.	*I don't like coffee.*

To talk about somebody else's likes and dislikes, use **le/les** (form.) before **gusta (-n)**. (See page 32 for more help with indirect pronouns.)

1 Asuntos personales *Personal matters*

¡OTRA VEZ!

● *Activity:* **1** ¿Qué te gusta? *What do you like?*
Example: Me gusta el café – *I like coffee.*

---

2 ¿Cuales son sus gustos? *What are his likes and dislikes?*
Example: Le gusta el vino – *He likes wine.*

LA FAMILIA
FAMILY

el árbol
  genealógico   *family tree*
los parientes   *relations*

los parientes
  cercanos   *close relations*
los parientes
  lejanos   *distant relations*

1 Asuntos personales *Personal matters*

materno;
  por parte
  de madre
	maternal;
	  on the mother's
	  side of the family
		el tío
		la tía
			uncle
			aunt

paterno;
  por parte
  de padre
	paternal;
	  on the father's
	  side
		el hijo
		el yerno
		la hija
		la nuera
			son
			son-in-law
			daughter
			daughter-in-law

los bisabuelos la bisabuela el bisabuelo	*great grandparents* *great grandmother* *great grandfather*	el hermano los hermanos el cuñado la hermana	*brother* *brothers and sisters* *brother-in-law* *sister*
los abuelos la abuela la abuelita el abuelo el abuelito el nieto/la nieta	*grandparents* *grandmother* *grandma* *grandfather* *grandpa* *grandson / daughter*	la cuñada el hermanastro la hermanastra el primo/la prima	*sister-in-law* *half-brother* *half-sister* *cousin*
los padres la madre la mamá la madrasta la suegra	*parents* *mother* *mum* *stepmother* *mother-in-law*	el/la adulto-a el/la adolescente el/la joven el/la niño-a los niños el bebé los padrinos la madrina el padrino el/la ahijado-a	*adult* *adolescent* *teenager* *child* *children* *baby* *godparents* *godmother* *godfather* *godchild*
el padre el papá el padrastro el suegro	*father* *dad* *stepfather* *father-in-law*		

Me gusta/No me gusta (alguien)	*I like / dislike (someone)*
Me llevo bien/mal con (alguien)	*I get on well / badly with (someone)*
No aguanto a (alguien)	*I can't stand (someone)*

los/las
  gemelos-as
el hermano
  mayor
la hermana
  menor
el/la hijo-a
  único-a
el/la huérfano-a
el matrimonio
	identical twins
	
	older brother
	
	younger sister
	
	only child
	orphan
	married couple
		los/las
		  mellizos-as
		adoptado-a
		una fotografía
		un álbum
		  de fotos
		Esta es una
		  foto de mi . . .
			twins
			adopted
			photograph
			
			photograph album
			Here is a photo
			  of my . . .

LOS ANIMALES
DOMÉSTICOS
PETS

¡Cuidado con el perro!
Beware of the dog!

el perro	*dog*
el caniche	*poodle*
el labrador	*labrador*
el pastor alemán	*alsatian*
el pastor escocés/	
el collie	*collie*
el perro de caza	*hunting dog*
el perro	
guardián	*guard dog*
el perro-guía	*guide dog*
el cesto	
del perro	*dog box; basket*
el collar	*collar*
la comida	*food*
la correa	*lead*
el hueso	*bone*
la caca de perro	*dog dirt*

el canario	*canary*
el pájaro	*bird*
el periquito	*budgerigar*
la jaula	*cage*
el alpiste	*birdseed*
el pez de colores	*gold fish*
el pez tropical	*tropical fish*
el acuario	*aquarium*
el estanque	*pond*
el conejillo	
de Indias	*guinea pig*
el conejo	*rabbit*
el gato	*cat*
el hámster	*hamster*
el loro	*parrot*
el ratón	*mouse*
la tortuga	*tortoise*
coger; atrapar	*to catch*
dar de beber a	*to give water to*
dar de comer a	*to feed*
limpiar	*to clean (out)*
llevar de paseo a	*to exercise*
sacar a pasear a	*to take for a walk*

2 El nacimiento, el matrimonio y la muerte
Birth, marriage and death

¡FELIZ CUMPLEAÑOS!
HAPPY BIRTHDAY!

El alumbramiento *Childbirth*

el nacimiento	*birth*
el cumpleaños	*birthday*
la fecha de nacimiento	*date of birth*
el bebé	*baby*
el niño	*boy*
la niña	*girl*
la cesárea	*caesarian*
la comadrona	*midwife*
las contracciones	*contractions*
el embarazo	*pregnancy*
el feto	*foetus*
los fórceps	*forceps*
la matriz	*womb*

el/la médico	*doctor*
el parto	*labour; delivery*
el parto sin dolor	*natural birth*
varón/hembra	*male / female*
el bautismo	*baptism*
el bautizo	*christening*
la madrina	*godmother*
el nombre	*name*
el padrino	*godfather*
los padrinos	*godparents*
un regalo; un obsequio	*present; gift*

El bebé *Baby*

el bebé	*baby*
los padres	*parents*
la niñera	*child minder*
un-a canguro	*baby sitter*

¿Puedes darme . . . ?	*Can I have the . . . ?*
Dáme . . .	*Pass me the . . .*
Necesito . . .	*I need the . . .*
el andador	*baby walker*
el babero	*bib*
la bañera del bebé	*baby's bath*
el biberón	*baby's bottle*
la camiseta	*vest*
la canción de cuna	*lullaby*
la caja de música	*musical chimes; music box*
el chupete	*dummy*
el cochecito	*pram*
la comida para niños/potitos	*baby food*
la cuna	*cot*
el edredón	*quilt*
la manta	*cot blanket*
la sábana de cuna	*cot sheet*
el imperdible	*nappy pin*

2 El nacimiento, el matrimonio y la muerte
Birth, marriage and death

los juguetes	toys
la leche	milk
la leche en polvo	powdered milk
la manopla	cloth
el orinal	potty
los pañales	nappies
los pañales de usar y tirar; dodotis	disposable nappies
el pijama	sleeping suit
la sillita	push chair
la sillita de coche	car seat
el sonajero	rattle
la toalla	towel
las toallitas húmedas	wipes
la trona	high chair

nacer	to be born	destetar	to wean
el/ella nació . . .	he / she was born . . .	dormirse/	to get to sleep /
tener un bebé	to have a baby	despertarse	to wake up
Ella ha tenido		echar los	
un bebé.	She has had a baby.	dientes	to teethe
		eructar	to burp
alimentar	to feed	hervir/es-	
bañar	to bath	terilizar	to boil / sterilise
cambiar el		limpiar	to wipe
pañal	to change the	llorar	to cry
	nappy	mecer	to rock
crecer	to grow	sacar de paseo	to take for a walk
criar con		sonreír	to smile
biberón	to bottle feed		
dar el pecho a	to breast feed		

El/ella . . .	He / she . . .
llora mucho	cries a lot
no duerme	doesn't sleep
Necesito . . .	I need . . .
crema para . . .	cream for . . .
un culito escocido	a sore bottom
las quemaduras de sol	sunburn

2 El nacimiento, el matrimonio y la muerte
Birth, marriage and death

---

medicina para . . .
    la indigestión
    la dentición
    la tos

medicine for . . .
    indigestion
    teething
    a cough

¿Cuándo le toca una toma?
¿Cuándo le toca dormir?

When should he/she be fed?
When should he/she have a sleep?

¡OTRA VEZ!

● *Activity:* ¡Ayuda a Mamá! ¿Qué es lo que no encuentra?
Help mother! What can't she find?

2 El nacimiento, el matrimonio y la muerte
Birth, marriage and death

CRECIENDO
GROWING UP

el/la crío-a	*infant*
el/la pequeñito-a	*toddler*
el/la niño-a	*child*
el/la adolescente	*adolescent*
la pubertad	*puberty*
la bicicleta	*bicycle*
la caja de los juguetes	*toy box*
el cassette para niños	*children's cassette*
el coche de juguete	*toy car*
el cochecito	*push chair*
las construcciones	*building bricks*
los juegos de aprendizaje	*early learning games*
los juguetes	*toys*
el libro de cuentos para niños	*children's story book*
el rompecabezas	*jigsaw*
los trenes/coches en miniatura	*model trains / cars*
el triciclo	*tricycle*
el video para niños	*children's video*

¿Hay . . .?	*Is there a . . .?*
un columpio	*swing*
un parque infantil	*children's playground*
una rueda; un tiovivo	*roundabout*
un tobogán	*slide*

sentarse	*to sit up*
gatear	*to crawl*
caerse	*to fall*
aprender a andar	*to learn to walk*
aprender a hablar	*to learn to talk*
jugar	*to play*
crecer	*to grow up*

¿Es . . .?	*Is it . . .?*
seguro-a	*safe*
peligroso-a	*dangerous*
apropiado-a para niños de (3) años	*suitable for (3) year olds*

2 El nacimiento, el matrimonio y la muerte
Birth, marriage and death

EL AMOR Y EL MATRIMONIO
LOVE AND MARRIAGE

¡Te quiero!   *I love you!*

el amigo/novio	boy friend
la amiga/novia	girl friend
el compromiso	engagement
el/la prometido-a	fiancé-e
el cónyuge; la pareja	partner
la petición de mano	proposal
el/la amante	lover
el heterosexual	heterosexual
el homosexual; el gay	homosexual
la lesbiana	lesbian

quererse	to love each other
enamorarse	to fall in love
prometerse	to get engaged
salir juntos	to go out together
acostarse juntos	to sleep together
tener relaciones sexuales con ...	to have sex with ...

EL MATRIMONIO
MARRIAGE

¡Felicidades!
Congratulations!

el anillo	ring
el aniversario de boda	wedding anniversary
la boda	wedding
la boda civil	civil marriage
las bodas de plata/de oro	silver / gold wedding
la boda por la iglesia	church wedding
la ceremonia	ceremony
la dama de honor	maid of honour
el día de la boda	wedding-day
la invitación	invitation
la luna de miel	honeymoon
el marido	husband
la mujer; esposa	wife
la novia	bride
el novio	bridegroom
el padrino/ la madrino	best man / matron of honour
el paje	page boy
la partida de casamiento	certificate
los recién casados	newly-weds
el regalo de boda	wedding present
el registro civil	registry office
el traje de novia	wedding dress

EL ESTADO CIVIL
MARITAL STATUS

Soy ...	I am ...
soltero-a	single

Estoy ...	I am ...
casado-a	married
divorciado-a	divorced
separado-a	separated
viviendo con ...	living with ...

2 El nacimiento, el matrimonio y la muerte
Birth, marriage and death

el apellido de soltera	*maiden name*	el divorcio	*divorce*
el apellido de casada	*married name*	casarse	*to get married*
la separación	*separation*	separarse	*to get separated*
		divorciarse	*to get divorced*

LA MUERTE   *DEATH*

Mi . . . ha muerto.	*My . . . has died.*
marido	*husband*
mujer	*wife*
amigo-a	*friend*
Estoy . . .	*I am (a) . . .*
desconsolado-a	*bereaved*
viuda	*widow*
viudo	*widower*

EL FUNERAL
The funeral

el ataúd	*coffin*	dar un ataque al corazón	*to have a heart attack*
el cementerio	*cemetery*	dar el pésame	*to convey one's condolences*
el duelo	*mourners*		
el entierro	*burial*	enterrar	*to bury*
la incineración	*cremation*	estar de luto	*to mourn*
el luto	*mourning*	matarse	*to kill oneself*
el testamento	*will*	morir en un accidente	*to be killed in an accident*
la tumba	*grave*	ser envenenado	*to be poisoned*
		suicidarse	*to commit suicide*
morirse	*to die*	tener cáncer	*to have cancer*
dar una apoplejía	*to have a stroke*		
		el/la heredero-a	*heir / heiress*
		heredar	*to inherit*

Deseo expresarle mi más sentido pésame.	*I would like to convey my condolences.*
Reciba mi más sincero pésame por tan dolorosa pérdida.	*I am very sorry to learn of your sad loss.*

3 La ropa y la moda *Clothes and fashion*

LA MODA
FASHION

la casa de modas	*fashion house*
el/la cliente	*client*
el/la comentarista	*commentator*
el desfile de modelos	*fashion show*
el/la diseñador-a	*designer*
el/la fotógrafo	*photographer*
el/la modelo	*model*
el modisto	*couturier*
la pasarela	*cat walk*
la revista de modas	*fashion magazine*

LA ROPA
CLOTHES

la bata; el batín	*dressing gown*
la blusa	*blouse*
los calcetines	*socks*
la camisa	*shirt*
la camisa polo	*polo shirt*
la camiseta	*T-shirt*
el camisón	*nightdress*
el chaleco	*waistcoat*
el chandal	*track suit*
el cinturón	*belt*
la corbata	*tie*
el delantal	*apron*
el esmoquin	*dinner jacket*
la falda	*skirt*
las medias	*stockings*
los pantalones	*trousers*
los pantalones cortos	*shorts*
los pantis	*tights*
el pijama	*pyjamas*
la rebeca	*cardigan*
la sudadera	*sweat shirt*

el suéter	*jumper*
el suéter de cuello cisne	*roll neck sweater*
los tirantes	*braces*
el traje	*suit*
el traje de noche	*evening dress*
el uniforme	*uniform*
los vaqueros; tejanos	*jeans*
el vestido	*dress*

La ropa interior   *Underwear*

el body	*body*
las bragas	*knickers*
los calzoncillos	*underpants; briefs*
la camiseta	*vest*
la combinación	*slip*
la faja	*girdle*
el liguero	*suspender belt*
la media combinación	*underskirt*
el sujetador	*bra*

La ropa de abrigo   *Outerwear*

el abrigo	*coat*
el anorak	*anorak*
la bufanda	*scarf*
la capucha	*hood*
la chaqueta	*jacket*
la gabardina	*rain coat*
la gorra	*cap*
la gorra de béisbol	*baseball cap*
el gorro de lana	*woolly hat*
los guantes	*gloves*
el impermeable	*mac*
el pañuelo de cabeza	*headscarf*
el paraguas	*umbrella*
el sombrero	*hat*

3 La ropa y la moda *Clothes and fashion*

La ropa de baño *Swimwear*

el bañador	*swimsuit*
el bikini	*bikini*
el gorro de baño	*swim hat*
el pantalón de baño	*trunks*
el traje de baño	*swimming costume*

EL CALZADO
FOOTWEAR

las aletas	*flippers*
las botas	*boots*
las botas de esquiar	*ski boots*
las botas de fútbol	*football boots*
las botas de goma	*rubber boots*

los cordones	*laces*
las sandalias	*sandals*
las zapatillas	*slippers*
las zapatillas de deporte	*trainers*
los zapatos	*shoes*
los zapatos con cordones	*lace-ups*
los zapatos de tacón alto	*high heeled shoes*

cambiarse	*to change*
llevar	*to wear*
ponerse	*to put on*
probarse	*to try . . . on*
quitarse	*to take off*
quitarse la ropa	*to get undressed*
vestirse	*to get dressed*

¡OTRA VEZ!

● Activity: ¿Qué llevan? *What are they wearing?*

---

3 **La ropa y la moda** *Clothes and fashion*

PARTES DE LAS PRENDAS
PARTS OF THE GARMENTS

el bolsillo	*pocket*
la costura	*seam*
el cuello	*collar*
el cuerpo	*bodice*
el dobladillo	*hem*
el doblez	*turn-up*
la manga	*sleeve*
el ojal	*buttonhole*
el pliegue	*pleat*
el puño	*cuff*
la sisa	*dart*
la solapa	*lapel*

Tejidos *Materials*

de algodón	*cotton*
de encaje	*lace*
de fieltro	*felt*
de goma	*rubber*
de lana	*wool*
de lino	*linen*
de nilón	*nylon*
de plástico	*plastic*
de poliéster	*polyester*
de punto	*knitted*
de raso	*satin*
de seda	*silk*
de tela vaquera	*denim*
de terciopelo	*velvet*
de tweed	*tweed*

PIELES
FURS/LEATHER

de ante	*suede*
de charol	*patent leather*
de cuero	*leather*
de napa	*imitation leather*
de piel	*fur/leather*

de piel falsa	*artificial fur*
de visón	*mink*

LA COSTURA
SEWING

¡A coser!	*Sew it up!*
la aguja	*needle*
el alfiler	*pin*
el botón	*button*
el corchete	*fastener*
la cremallera	*zip*
el dedal	*thimble*
el hilo	*thread*
el imperdible	*safety pin*
la máquina de coser	*sewing machine*
el metro	*measuring tape*
el patrón	*pattern*
la puntada	*stitch*
las tijeras	*scissors*

ADJETIVOS ÚTILES
USEFUL ADJECTIVES

ajustado-a	*tight fitting*
ancho-a	*loose*
arrugado-a	*crumpled*
clásico-a	*classical*
con dibujo/liso-a	*patterned/plain*
confeccionado-a	*off-the-peg*
de cuadros	*checked*
de cuadros escoceses	*tartan*
elegante	*smart*
estampado-a	*printed*
estrecho-a	*tight*
de etiqueta	*formal*
de flores	*floral*
largo-a/corto-a	*long/short*
de lunares	*spotted*
de moda	*fashionable*

3 La ropa y la moda *Clothes and fashion*

muy holgado-a	*baggy*
no combina bien	*ill-matching*
pasado-a de moda	*old fashioned*
plisado-a	*pleated*
de rayas	*striped*
de sport	*casual*

EL CUIDADO DE LA ROPA
CLOTHES CARE

la percha	*coat hanger*
la percha para faldas	*skirt hanger*
el perchero	*coatstand*
la plancha	*iron*
la plancha de vapor	*steam iron*

la prensa para pantalones	*trouser press*
acortar	*to shorten*
alargar	*to lengthen*
arreglar	*to alter*
cambiar	*to change*
colgar	*to hang up*
coser	*to sew*
hacer	*to make*
limpiar	*to clean*
limpiar en seco	*to dry clean*
planchar	*to iron*
rasgarse	*to tear*
teñir	*to stain*
unir	*to tie*
zurcir	*to mend*

¡OTRA VEZ!

● *Activity:* ¿Qué están poniendo en la maleta? *What are they packing?*

59

3 La ropa y la moda *Clothes and fashion*

¿Lavar o limpiar en seco?	*Wash or dry clean?*
Símbolos de lavado	*Washing symbols*
Limpieza en seco; lavar en seco	*Dry clean only*
Lavado a mano	*Handwash only*
Lavar aparte	*Wash separately*
Usar agua templada (30°C)	*Use tepid water (30°C)*
No usar secadora	*Do not tumble dry*
No usar lejía	*Do not use bleach*
No planchar	*Do not iron*
Planchado a temperatura media	*Use only cool iron*
Extender húmedo	*Spread out to dry*
No mantener en remojo	*Do not soak*
No usar detergente	*Do not use detergent*
Usar jabón neutro	*Use neutral soap*
Limpiar con trapo húmedo	*Wipe with a damp cloth*
Puede usar secadora	*Can be tumble dried*
Aclarar sin retorcer	*Rinse without wringing*

COMPLEMENTOS
ACCESSORIES

el bolso de bandolera	*shoulder bag*
el bolso de mano	*handbag*
el chal	*shawl*
el cinturón	*belt*
los guantes	*gloves*
el monedero	*purse*
el pañuelo	*scarf*
el paraguas	*umbrella*
el reloj (de pulsera)	*watch*

JOYAS Y PERFUMES
JEWELLERY AND PERFUME

el alfiler de corbata	*tie pin*
el anillo	*ring*
la alianza	*wedding ring*
el anillo de compromiso	*engagement ring*
el anillo de sello	*signet ring*
la bisutería	*costume jewellery*
el broche	*brooch*
el colgante	*pendant*
el collar	*necklace*
la cruz	*cross*
la diadema	*tiara*
los gemelos	*cuff links*
los pendientes	*earrings*
la pulsera	*bracelet*

Metales y piedras preciosas y semi-preciosas
Metals and precious and semi-precious stones

¡Un brillante es para siempre!
Diamonds are forever.

la amatista	*amethyst*
el bronce	*bronze*

3 La ropa y la moda *Clothes and fashion*

el cobre	*copper*		el zafiro	*sapphire*
el coral	*coral*			
el cristal	*crystal*		el quilate	*carat*
el diamante;			la talla	*cut*
el brillante	*diamond*			

el esmalte	*enamel*
la esmeralda	*emerald*
el lapislázuli	*lapis lazuli*
el ópalo	*opal*
el oro	*gold*
la perla	*pearl*
la plata	*silver*
el platino	*platinum*
el rubí	*ruby*

Perfumes *Perfume*

el agua de colonia	*toilet water; eau de cologne*
de flores	*flowery*
la fragancia	*scent*
de lavanda	*lavender*
el vaporizador	*spray*

¡OTRA VEZ!

● *Activity:* ¿Qué van a comprar? *What are they going to buy?*

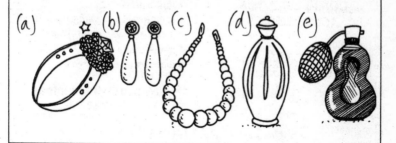

(a) (b) (c) (d) (e)

4 La comida y la bebida *Food and drink*

COMPUESTOS DE LOS ALIMENTOS: INGREDIENTES Y PREPARACIÓN
FOODSTUFFS AND FOOD PREPARATION

las calorías	*calories*
el carbohidrato	*carbohydrate*
la fibra	*fibre*
la grasa	*fat*
los minerales	*minerals*
las proteínas	*proteins*
las vitaminas	*vitamins*
integral	*wholemeal*
mono-insaturado-a	*monounsaturated*
orgánico-a	*organic*
poliinsaturado-a	*polyunsaturated*
Sin colorantes ni conservantes	*No artificial colouring or preservatives*
líquido-a	*liquid*
sólido-a	*solid*
¡(No) es sano!	*It's good / bad for you!*
la cocina	*cooking* (la cuisine)
la cocinera	*cook*
la gastronomía	*gastronomy*
el jefe de cocina	*chef*
la receta	*recipe*

LOS INGREDIENTES
COOKING INGREDIENTS

el azúcar	*sugar*
el azúcar morena	*brown sugar*
el bicarbonato sódico	*bicarbonate of soda*

la harina	*flour*
la harina de maíz	*cornflour*
la harina integral	*wholemeal flour*
la levadura	*yeast*
la sal fina	*fine salt*
la sal gorda	*coarse salt*
la sal marina	*sea salt*

Las grasas *Fat*

el aceite	*oil*
el aceite de oliva	*olive oil*
el aceite de girasol	*sunflower oil*
la manteca	*animal fat*
la mantequilla	*butter*
la margarina	*margarine*

Los productos lácteos *Dairy goods*

la leche	*milk*
la mantequilla	*butter*
la nata	*cream*
el queso	*cheese*
cabrales	*de cabrales (Spanish blue cheese)*
de bola	*Edam type cheese*
manchego	*manchego (ewe's milk cheese)*
el yogur	*yoghurt*
semi-descremado-a	*half fat*

4 La comida y la bebida *Food and drink*

El huevo *Egg*

la yema	*egg yolk*
la clara del huevo	*egg white*

Los frutos secos
Dried fruit and nuts

la almendra	*almond*
la avellana	*hazelnut*
el cacahuete	*peanut*
el coco	*coconut*
el dátil	*date*
el higo	*fig*
la nuez	*walnut*
la pasa	*raisin; sultana*
la pipa	*sunflower seed*
el pistacho	*pistachio*

Las legumbres *Pulses*

las alubias blancas	*butter beans*
las alubias pintas	*red kidney beans*
los garbanzos	*chick peas*
las lentejas	*lentils*
el arroz	*rice*
los espaguetis	*spaghetti*
la pasta	*pasta*

Los utensilios de cocina
Cooking utensils

el abrebotellas	*bottle opener*
el abrelatas	*tin opener*
el afilador de cuchillos	*knife sharpener*
la bandeja de horno	*baking tray*
el batidor	*whisk*
el cazo	*saucepan*
el colador	*sieve*
la cuchara de madera	*wooden spoon*
el cuchillo de cocina	*kitchen knife*
el cuenco	*bowl*
el escurridor	*colander*
los guantes para el horno	*oven gloves*
el minipimer	*hand held food processor*
el molde desmontable para pastel	*cake tin*
el molinillo de café	*coffee grinder*
la parrilla	*griddle*
el peso	*weighing scales*
el rodillo	*rolling pin*
el sacacorchos	*corkscrew*
la sartén	*frying pan*
la tabla de picar	*chopping board*
las tijeras	*scissors*
el ajuste	*setting*
el avisador	*timer*
la batidora	*mixer*
la cafetera	*coffee machine*
el grill	*grill*
el quemador	*hob*
el termostato	*thermostat*
el tostador	*toaster*

Las hierbas y las especias
Herbs and spices

Las hierbas aromáticas	**Herbs**
la albahaca	*basil*
el anís	*aniseed*
el azafrán	*saffron*
el eneldo	*dill*
el estragón	*tarragon*
la hierbabuena	*mint*
el laurel	*bayleaves*

4 La comida y la bebida *Food and drink*

el orégano	*oregano*	el jengibre	*ginger*
el perejil	*parsley*	la nuez moscada	*nutmeg*
el romero	*rosemary*	el pimentón	*paprika*
la salvia	*sage*	la pimienta	*pepper*
el tomillo	*thyme*		
		el ajo	*garlic*
Las especias	**Spices**	el edulcorante	*artificial sweetener*
la canela	*cinnamon*	la miel	*honey*
el clavo	*clove*	la mostaza	*mustard*
el comino	*cumin*	la vainilla	*vanilla*

LOS SABORES   *TASTE AND FLAVOUR*

Mmm . . . ¡Me gusta!
¡Está riquísimo!
¡No me gusta! ¡Está . . .!

Mmmmm . . . I like it!
It's delicious!
I don't like it. It's . . .!

agrio-a	*sour*	incomible	*inedible*
ahumado-a	*smoked*	insípido-a	*tasteless*
amargo-a	*bitter*	sabroso-a	*tasty*
delicioso-a;		salado-a	*salted*
rico-a	*delicious*	seco-a	*dried*
dulce	*sweet*	soso-a	*bland; lacking salt*
duro-a	*tough; stale* (bread)	tierno-a	*tender*

VERBOS ÚTILES
USEFUL VERBS

		gratinar	*to cook au gratin*
		guisar	*to stew*
		hervir	*to boil*
asar	*to bake; roast*	hornear	*to roast*
asar a la parrilla	*to grill*	lavar	*to wash*
batir	*to beat*	limpiar	*to clean*
brasear	*to braise*	mezclar	*to mix*
calentar	*to heat*	pelar	*to peel*
cocer	*to cook*	picar	*to chop; mince*
cocer al vapor	*to steam*	pringar	*to baste*
colar	*to strain*	rellenar	*to stuff; fill*
cortar	*to cut*	remover	*to stir*
derretir	*to melt*	sazonar	*to season*
enfriar	*to cool*	secar	*to dry*
estofar	*to stew*	tostar	*to toast*
freír	*to fry*	triturar	*to grind; crush*

4 La comida y la bebida *Food and drink*

FRUTA Y VERDURA *FRUIT AND VEGETABLES*

¡Alimentación sana, natural y equilibrada!	*Healthy Eating! Vitamins! Fibre!*

La fruta *Fruit*

la compota de fruta	*fruit purée*	el mango	*mango*
		la manzana	*apple*
la macedonia de frutas	*fruit salad*	el melocotón	*peach*
		el melón	*melon*
la mermelada	*jam*	el membrillo	*quince*
		la mora	*blackberry*
el aguacate	*avocado*	la naranja	*orange*
el albaricoque	*apricot*	el níspero	*medlar*
la cereza	*cherry*	la pera	*pear*
la chirimoya	*custard apple*	la piña	*pineapple*
la ciruela	*plum*	el plátano	*banana*
la frambuesa	*raspberry*	el pomelo	*grapefruit*
la fresa	*strawberry*	la sandía	*watermelon*
la granada	*pomegranite*	las uvas	*grapes*
el higo	*fig*		
el kiwi	*kiwi*	pelar	*to peel*
la lima	*lime*	la piel	*skin*
el limón	*lemon*	las pipas	*pips*
la mandarina	*mandarin orange*	las semillas	*seeds*
		trocear	*to cut up*

Las verduras *Vegetables*

¡Lavar bien antes de consumirlas!	*Wash before eating!*

cocido-a	*cooked*	el brécol	*broccoli*
crudo-a	*raw*	el calabacín	*courgette*
rallado-a	*grated*	la cebolla	*onion*
		el champiñón; la seta	*mushroom*
la aceituna	*olive*		
la alcachofa	*artichoke*	la col; el repollo	*cabbage*
el ajo	*garlic*	la col de Bruselas	*Brussel sprouts*
el apio	*celery*		
la berenjena	*aubergine*	la col roja	*red cabbage*

4 La comida y la bebida *Food and drink*

la coliflor	*cauliflower*	la patata	*potato*
los guisantes	*peas*	el pimiento	*pepper*
los espárragos	*asparagus*	el puerro	*leek*
las espinacas	*spinach*	la remolacha	*beetroot*
las habas	*broad beans*	la zanahoria	*carrot*
la habichuela	*runner bean*		
la judía verde	*green bean*	la lechuga	*lettuce*
el nabo	*turnip*	el pepino	*cucumber*
		el tomate	*tomato*

4 La comida y la bebida *Food and drink*

LAS BEBIDAS
DRINKS

Las bebidas calientes
Hot drinks

una taza de . . .	*a cup of . . .*
con leche	*with milk*
con limón	*with lemon*
con nata	*with cream*
el azúcar	*sugar*
el edulcorante	*sweetener*
la cucharilla	*teaspoon*
el platillo	*saucer*

El té — **Tea**

la bolsa de té	*tea-bag*
la manzanilla	*camomile tea*
la tisana	*tisane*

El café — **Coffee**

el café con leche	*white coffee*
el café instantáneo	*instant coffee*
el café solo	*black coffee*
el cortado	*small coffee with a little milk*
el descafeinado	*decaffeinated coffee*
el chocolate caliente	*hot chocolate*

Los refrescos *Cold drinks*

una botella	*a bottle*
un brik	*a carton*
una lata	*a can*
un vaso	*a glass*
el agua	*water*
el agua mineral sin gas	*still mineral water*

el agua mineral con gas	*carbonated mineral water*
el batido (de fresa)	*milk shake (strawberry)*
la coca-cola	*coca cola*
la granizada (de limón)	*iced drink (lemon)*
la horchata	*tiger nut milk*
un refresco de limón	*lemonade*
un refresco de naranja	*orangeade*
la tónica	*tonic*
un zumo	*fruit juice*
de manzana	*apple*
de naranja	*orange*
de tomate	*tomato*

¡Salud! *Cheers!*

El alcohol — **Alcohol**

la cerveza	*beer (lager)*
la cerveza negra	*dark beer (stout)*
la cerveza sin alcohol	*alcohol free beer*
el vino . . .	*. . . wine*
tinto	*red*
blanco	*white*
rosado	*rosé*
el cava	*cava (Spanish sparkling wine)*
el champán	*champagne*
el fino	*dry sherry*
la manzanilla	*manzanilla*
el vino de mesa	*table wine*
el vino dulce/seco	*sweet / dry wine*
el coñac	*brandy; cognac*
el ron	*rum*
la sangría	*sangria*
el whisky	*whisky*
el vodka	*vodka*
el cubata	*rum and coke*

el tinto de verano	*red wine and carbonated water*	con/sin hielo	*with / without ice*
		beber; tomar	*to drink*
con/sin limón	*with / without lemon*	sorber	*to sip*

¡OTRA VEZ!

● *Activity:* What would you say to order these drinks?

Quisiera . . .   I would like . . .

4 La comida y la bebida *Food and drink*

LAS COMIDAS
MEALS

¡Que aproveche!
Enjoy your meal!

el almuerzo	*lunch*
la cena	*dinner; supper*
el desayuno	*breakfast*
la merienda	*tea; afternoon snack*
la tapa	*tapa; small snack*

El desayuno *Breakfast*

los cereales	*cereal*
las galletas	*biscuits*
la mantequilla	*butter*
la margarina	*margarine*
la mermelada	*jam*
la miel	*honey*
la nata	*cream*
el pomelo	*grapefruit*
una tostada	*a piece of toast*
el zumo de naranja	*orange juice*

El almuerzo y la cena *Lunch and dinner*

las patatas . . .	*. . . potatoes*
al horno	*baked*
asadas	*roast*
cocidas	*boiled*
fritas	*chips*
el puré de patatas	*creamed potatoes*

las verduras . . .	*. . . vegetables*
(See also: *Fruit and vegetables*, page 65.)	
cocidas	*cooked*
crudas	*raw*
hervidas	*boiled*
rehogadas	*sautéed*

los huevos . . .	*. . . eggs*
duros	*hard boiled*
fritos	*fried*
pasados por agua	*soft boiled*
revueltos	*scrambled*

la tortilla	*omelette*
la tortilla de patatas	*potato omelette*
la tortilla francesa	*plain omelette*

4 La comida y la bebida *Food and drink*

LA COMIDA
FOOD
La carne *Meat*

el cerdo	*pork*
el cordero	*lamb*
la ternera	*beef*
la ternera de Ávila	*veal*
la carne picada	*minced meat*
la salchicha	*sausage*

Las aves *Poultry*

la oca	*goose*
el pato	*duck*
el pavo	*turkey*
el pollo	*chicken*

La caza *Game*

el conejo	*rabbit*
la cordoniz	*quail*
el faisán	*pheasant*
la liebre	*hare*
la perdiz	*partridge*
el venado	*venison*

Los fiambres
Cooked meat; charcuterie

el beicon	*bacon*
el chorizo	*chorizo*
el foie-gras	*paté*
el jamón de York	*boiled ham*
el jamón serrano	*raw ham*
el salami	*salami*
el salchichón	*salami-type sausage*
la costilla	*rib*

la chuleta	*chop*
el filete	*steak*
la pierna	*leg*
el pescado	*fish*

(See also page 112)

el pescado ahumado	*smoked fish*

El pan *Bread*

la barra	*baguette*
el croissant	*croissant*
las galletas saladas	*crackers*
el pan integral	*wholemeal bread*
el pan rallado	*breadcrumbs*
el panecillo/ la viena	*bread roll*
el bocadillo	*sandwich (roll)*
el sándwich; el emparedado	*sandwich (English typ*

No tomo carne/ productos lácteos.	*I don't eat meat / dairy products.*
Soy vegetariano-a.	*I am a vegetarian.*
Me encanta . . .	*I love . . .*
Mi . . . favorito-a es . . .	*My favourite . . . is . . .*

PONER LA MESA
LAYING THE TABLE

la cuchara	*spoon*
el cuchillo	*knife*
el mantel	*tablecloth*
la servilleta	*napkin*
el tenedor	*fork*
el salvamanteles	*place mat*
la copa	*glass (for sherry, champagne, etc.)*

4 La comida y la bebida *Food and drink*

el cuenco	*bowl*
la jarra	*jug*
el platillo	*saucer*
el plato	*plate; dish*
la taza	*cup*
el vaso	*glass* (for milk, water etc.)

Los condimentos
Condiments

el aceite	*oil*
la mostaza	*mustard*
la pimienta	*pepper*
la sal	*salt*
el vinagre	*vinegar*
el kétchup	*tomato sauce*
la mayonesa	*mayonnaise*

EXPRESIONES ÚTILES
USEFUL EXPRESSIONS

Está en . . .	*It's in / on . . .*
el cajón	*the drawer*
el armarito	*the wallcupboard*
la nevera	*the fridge*
el lavavajillas	*the dishwasher*
la repisa	*the shelf*
¡Que aproveche!	*Enjoy your meal!* (Bon appétit!)
¡Igualmente!	*And you too!*
Me gusta . . .	*I like . . .*
No me gusta . . .	*I don't like . . .*
No puedo más.	*I'm full.*
Es demasiado.	*It's too much.*
Está . . .	*It's . . .*
soso-a	*bland; lacking salt*
demasiado agrio-a	*too sour*
demasiado caliente	*too hot*
demasiado dulce	*too sweet*
demasiado frío-a	*too cold*

4 La comida y la bebida *Food and drink*

COMER FUERA DE CASA
EATING OUT

¡Oiga, por favor!
Excuse me, please!

el bar	*bar*
el café	*café*
el comedor	*dining room; canteen*
la hamburgue-sería	*fast food restaurant*
la marisquería	*seafood bar / restaurant*
la pizzería	*pizzeria*
el restaurante	*restaurant*
el self service	*self-service*
la venta	*country inn*
el cenicero	*ashtray*
el cubierto	*place setting*
los cubiertos	*cutlery*
la mesa	*table*
el palillo	*tooth pick*
la salsa	*sauce*
la servilleta	*serviette*
la silla	*chair*

el camarero	*waiter*
la camarera	*waitress*
el sumiller	*wine waiter*
la cuenta	*bill*
el IVA	*VAT*
la propina	*tip*
el recibo	*receipt*
el servicio	*service charge*
la vuelta	*change*
la carta	*menu*
el menú del día	*menu of the day*
el primer plato	*first course*
los entremeses	*hors d'oeuvre*
la ensalada	*salad*
el plato principal	*main course*
el segundo plato	*second course*
el plato de pescado	*fish course*
el postre	*dessert*
el queso	*cheese*
la fruta	*fruit*
beber	*to drink*
comer	*to eat*
pagar	*to pay*
tomar	*to have* (food/drink)

Las tapas *Tapas*

Una tapa de . . .	A tapa of . . .
aceitunas	*olives*
bacalao con tomate	*cod in tomato sauce*
carne en salsa	*meat in sauce*
champiñón al ajillo	*mushrooms in garlic*
ensaladilla rusa	*potato & vegetable salad*
gambas	*prawns*
jamón	*raw ham*
queso	*cheese*
tortilla	*potato omelette*

4 La comida y la bebida *Food and drink*

Platos típicos
Typical dishes

el cocido	*chickpea and meat stew (Castilla)*
la fabada	*bean and pork stew (Asturias)*
el gazpacho	*cold tomato soup (Andalucía)*
la paella	*paella (Valencia)*

Aquí se come bien	*Here you eat well*
muy bien	*very well*
estupendamente	*very very well*
¡demasiado!	*too much!*
¿Me/nos trae la cuenta, por favor?	*Can I have the bill please?*
¿Podemos pagar por separado, por favor?	*Can we pay separately please?*
¿Está incluido el servicio?	*Is service included?*
¿Tengo que dejar propina?	*Should I leave a tip?*
¿Cuánto?	*How much?*
¡Para el bote!	*(said on giving a tip)*

¡OTRA VEZ!

● *Activity:* Dígale al camarero qué va a tomar. *Tell the waiter what you would like:*

de primero . . .	*as a starter*
de segundo . . .	*as main course*
de postre . . .	*for dessert*
para beber . . .	*to drink*

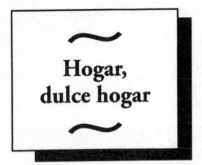

LA CASA Y LA VIVIENDA
HOUSING AND ACCOMMODATION

la casa . . .	*. . . house*
adosada	*terraced*
semi-adosada	*semi-detached*
unifamiliar	*detached*
la casa de campo	*cottage*
el chalet	*chalet*
la granja; el cortijo	*farm*
la villa	*villa*
la vivienda de protección oficial	*council house / flat*
una casa con . . .	*a house with . . .*
garaje	*a garage*
jardín	*a garden*
piscina	*a swimming pool*
plaza de aparcamiento	*a parking space*
el piso	*flat*
la casa/el piso alquilado-a	*rented house / flat*
la comunidad de propietarios	*owners' association*
el ascensor	*lift*
el portero electrónico	*answering device*
Soy/somos propietario(-s) de mi/nuestra vivienda.	*I / we own our own house.*

5 La casa, el hogar y el jardín *House, home and garden*

la agencia inmobiliaria	*estate agency*
el agente inmobiliario	*agent*
el/la comprador-a	*buyer*
la escritura	*deeds*
la hipoteca	*mortgage*
la llave	*key*
el préstamo	*loan*
la sociedad de préstamo inmobiliario	*building society*

la valoración	*valuation*
el/la vendedor-a	*seller*
el ático	*attic flat*
el barrio	*district; quarter*
el bloque de pisos	*block of flats*
el centro	*town / city centre*
el duplex	*split-level flat*
el/la inquilino-a	*tenant*
la urbanización	*housing estate*
el anuncio	*advertisement*

VENDO piso, zona Reina Mercedes, todo exterior, cinco dormitorios, 3 baños, aire acondicionado, estupendo estado, recién reformado, precio interesante. Telf. 95-4356562/91-3597091.

TRIANA (Los Remedios), 3 dormitorios, 6.500.000 contado. Teléfono 4340590.

SANTA Clara, ocasión, Nuevo Continente, 4 dormitorios, cocina con gran office, 2 cuartos de baño, 1 aseo, aparcamiento propio, club social, 18.500.000 pesetas. 4676458.

MADRID, San Bernardo 83. Particular. Exterior, lujo, amueblado, climatizado. 17.000.000. 96-5126165, tardes.

SIMON Verde, próxima construcción, dos últimos pareados, 607 m² parcela, 240 m² construidos. Aruncy. 4275067.

OCASION, Valencina, dos últimos chalets independientes, cuatro dormitorios, 400 m² parcela, 14.500.000. Aruncy. 4275067.

OPORTUNIDAD. Residencial Helios. Por traslado vendo casa. 4239503.

SANTA Eufemia, adosado, 5 minutos Sevilla, 3 dormitorios, uno doble, salón chimenea, 2 baños, 1 aseo, armarios empotrados, jardín privado, garaje 2 plazas, solárium, piscina común. Urge por traslado. Ocasión, 10.500.000, más 3.300.000 hipoteca. 4152637.

cerca de . . .	*near to . . .*
situado-a en el campo	*rural situation*
tranquilo-a	*quiet*
en el centro	*central location*
el aire acondicionado	*air conditioning*
el aislamiento	*insulation*
la calefacción central	*central heating*
el doble acristalamiento	*double glazing*
la insonorización	*sound proofing*

el carbón	*coal*
el combustible sólido	*solid fuel*
la electricidad	*electricity*
el gas	*gas*
la madera	*wood*
el petróleo	*oil*
alquilar	*to rent; let*
compartir	*to share*
comprar	*to buy*
pagar	*to pay*
tomar prestado	*to borrow*

5 La casa, el hogar y el jardín *House, home and garden*

Las partes de la casa
Parts of the house

el garaje	*garage*
la pared	*wall*
la persiana	*shutter*
la puerta	*door*
la puerta principal	*front door*
la reja	*window bars*
el suelo	*floor*
el techo	*ceiling*
el tejado	*roof*
la ventana	*window*
la verja	*gate*
la azotea	*terrace*
el bajo	*ground floor*
el balcón; la terraza	*balcony*
el desván	*attic; loft*
las escaleras	*stairs*
el patio	*patio*
el primer piso	*first floor*
el sótano	*basement; cellar*

Las habitaciones *Rooms*

la cocina	*kitchen*
el comedor	*dining room*
el cuarto de baño	*bathroom*
el cuarto de los niños	*play room*
el descansillo	*landing*
el dormitorio	*bedroom*
el estudio	*study*
la habitación de invitados	*spare room; guest room*
el lavadero	*laundry room*
el salón; la sala de estar	*lounge; sitting room*
el trastero	*boxroom*
el vestíbulo	*entrance hall*

¡OTRA VEZ!

● *Label each room in this flat.*

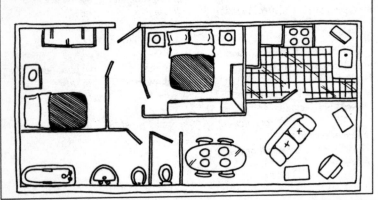

76

LOS MUEBLES Y LOS OBJETOS DE LA CASA
FURNITURE AND FURNISHINGS

la alfombra	*rug*	la lavadora	*washing machine*
la almohada	*pillow*	el lavavajillas	*dishwasher*
el armario	*wardrobe*	la librería	*bookcase*
el armario		la maceta	*plant pot*
empotrado	*fitted wardrobe*	la manta	*blanket*
el armarito	*wall cupboard*	el mantel	*tablecloth*
el aseo	*toilet*	la mecedora	*rocking chair*
el azulejo	*wall tile*	la mesa	*table*
la baldosa	*floor tile*	la mesa de café	*coffee table*
la bañera	*bath*	la mesita	
la cama	*bed*	de noche	*bedside table*
el cenicero	*ashtray*	el microondas	*microwave*
la clavija	*plug*	el módulo	
la cocina	*cooker*	de cocina	*kitchen unit*
el cojín	*cushion*	la moqueta	*carpet*
la colcha	*bedspread*	el ordenador	
el colchón	*mattress*	personal	*personal computer*
la cómoda	*chest of drawers*	el papel pintado	*wallpaper*
las cortinas	*curtains*	la plancha	*iron*
la cristalería	*glassware*	el quemador	*hob*
el cuadro	*picture; painting*	el radiador	*radiator*
la cubertería	*cutlery*	la radio	*radio*
la cuna	*cot*	el reloj de pared	*clock*
el edredón	*quilt; duvet*	la sábana	*sheet*
el enchufe	*socket*	la secadora	*tumble drier*
el equipo		la servilleta	*towel*
de música	*stereo*	la silla	*chair*
el espejo	*mirror*	el sillón	*armchair*
la estantería	*shelves*	el sofá	*sofa*
el florero	*vase*	el sofá cama	*sofa bed*
el fregadero	*sink*	la tabla	
el frigorífico	*fridge*	de planchar	*ironing board*
el grifo del agua		el taburete	*stool*
caliente/fría	*hot / cold water tap*	el televisor	*television*
el horno	*oven*	la toalla	*towel*
el interruptor	*switch*	el tostador	*toaster*
la lámpara	*lamp*	la trona	*high chair*
la lámpara		la vajilla	*crockery*
de pie	*standard lamp*	el vídeo	*video recorder*
el lavabo	*washbasin*	el visillo	*net curtain*

¡OTRA VEZ!

● *Activity:* ¿Qué les gustaría? ¿En qué habitación?
What would they like . . . for which room?

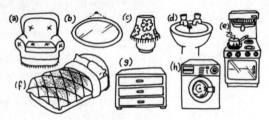

Me gustaría un-a . . . nuevo-a . . . para el/la . . .
I would like a new . . . for the . . .

LAS TAREAS DE LA CASA   HOUSEWORK

Mi marido no trabaja.
Es amo de casa.

My husband doesn't work. He's a house husband.

la aspiradora	*vacuum cleaner*
el cepillo;	
la escoba	*brush*
la cera para	
muebles	*furniture polish*
el cubo	*bucket*
el desinfectante	*disinfectant*

el detergente	*detergent*
la fregona	*mop*
la gamuza	*duster*
el limpiacristales	*window cleaner (detergent)*
el limpiahornos	*oven cleaner*
el papel	
higiénico	*toilet paper*

el producto de limpieza para . . .	
el cuarto de baño	*bathroom cleaner*
moquetas	*carpet cleaner*
suelos	*floor cleaner*

el recogedor	*dustpan*
la toalla de papel para la cocina	*kitchen roll*
el trapo	*cloth*
la limpiadora; la asistenta	*cleaner (person)*
barrer	*to sweep*
cargar/vaciar el lavavajillas	*to load / unload the dishwasher*
fregar los platos	*to do the washing up*
hacer las camas	*to make the beds*
lavar la ropa	*to do the washing / laundry*
limpiar	*to clean*
limpiar el polvo	*to dust*
limpiar las ventanas	*to clean the windows*
pasar la aspiradora	*to put the sweeper over*
planchar	*to do the ironing*
poner la mesa	*to lay the table*
sacar brillo	*to polish*
secar los platos	*to wipe (plates)*

EL JARDÍN *GARDEN*

la horticultura	*horticulture*
la jardinería	*gardening*
el abono	*manure*
el árbol	*tree*
el arbusto	*bush; shrub*
el arriate	*flower bed*
los bulbos	*bulbs*
el camino	*path*
el césped	*lawn*
el fertilizante	*fertiliser*

Las flores *Flowers*

el clavel	*carnation*
el crisantemo	*chrysanthemum*
el geranio	*geranium*
el girasol	*sunflower*
el lirio	*lily*
la margarita	*daisy*
la rosa	*rose*
la hierba	*grass*
las hierbas	*herbs*
la huerta	*vegetable garden*
el invernadero	*greenhouse*
la maceta	*plant pot*
la planta	*plant*
las semillas	*seeds*

Los útiles de jardinería *Garden tools*

el aspersor	*sprinkler*
la azada	*hoe*
la carretilla	*wheelbarrow*
el cortacésped	*lawn mower*
el desplantador	*trowel*
la horquilla	*fork*
la manguera	*hose-pipe*
la pala	*spade*
el rastrillo	*rake*
la regadera	*watering can*
la sierra	*saw*
la sierra de cadena	*chain saw*
las tijeras de podar	*secateurs*
las tijeras de jardín	*shears*

5 La casa, el hogar y el jardín *House, home and garden*

Los muebles de jardín
Garden furniture

la barbacoa	*barbecue*
el bebedero para pájaros	*bird bath*
el cobertizo	*garden shed*
el columpio	*swing*
la hamaca	*hammock*
la mesa de jardín	*garden table*
la piscina para niños	*paddling pool*
la silla de jardín	*garden chair*
la sombrilla	*sunshade*
el tobogán	*slide*
el toldo	*awning*
la tumbona	*deckchair*
al sol	*in the sun*
a la sombra	*in the shade*

El árbol *Tree*

la hoja	*leaf*
la raíz	*root*
la rama	*branch*
la ramita	*twig*
el tronco	*trunk*
los árboles frutales	*fruit trees*
la semilla	*seed*
la plántula	*seedling*
la hoja	*leaf*
la planta	*plant*
la flor	*flower*
en flor	*in blossom*
el fruto	*fruit*
abonar	*to fertilise*
cavar	*to dig*
coger	*to pick*
cortar la hierba/ el césped	*to cut the grass / the lawn*
cultivar	*to cultivate; grow*
desherbar	*to weed*
plantar	*to plant*
podar	*to prune*
regar	*to water; irrigate*
sembrar	*to sow*

6 El mundo del trabajo *Jobs and work*

LAS PROFESIONES Y LOS EMPLEOS
JOBS

Soy . . .	*I am a / an . . .*
El/ella es . . .	*He / she is a / an . . .*
abogado	*lawyer*
actor/actriz	*actor / actress*
agricultor	*farmer*
artista	*artist*
bibliotecario-a	*librarian*
bombero	*fireman*
camarero-a	*waitress / waitress*
cantante	*singer*
carnicero-a	*butcher*
cartero	*postman*
cirujano	*surgeon*
cocinero-a	*cook*
comprador-a; encargado-a de compras	*buyer*
conductor-a	*driver*
conductor de camiones; camionero	*lorry driver*
contable	*accountant*
contratista	*builder*
dentista	*dentist*
dependiente	*shop assistant*
director-a de empresa	*company director*
diseñador-a de modas	*fashion designer*
diseñador-a gráfico	*graphic designer*
diseñador-a industrial	*industrial designer*
electricista	*electrician*
empleado-a de banco	*bank employee*
enfermera	*nurse*
estudiante	*student*
farmacéutico-a	*chemist*
fisioterapeuta	*physiotherapist*
fontanero	*plumber*
funcionario-a (del estado)	*civil servant*
gerente	*manager*
guía de turismo	*tour guide*
hombre/mujer de negocios	*businessman / woman*
ingeniero	*engineer*
intérprete	*interpreter*
jardinero	*gardener*
limpiador-a	*cleaner*
marinero	*sailor*
mecánico	*mechanic*
médico	*doctor*
notario	*solicitor*
oficinista	*clerk*
operador-a de ordenadores	*computer operator*
panadero	*baker*
peluquero-a	*hairdresser*
periodista	*journalist*
pintor decorador	*painter and decorator*
policía	*policeman*
profesor-a	*teacher*
profesor-a de universidad	*lecturer*
químico (industrial)	*chemist*
radiógrafo	*radiographer*
recepcionista	*receptionist*
repartidor-a	*delivery man / woman*
representante; viajante	*sales representative*
secretario-a	*secretary*
soldado	*soldier*
taxista	*taxi driver*
telefonista	*telephonist*
traductor-a	*translator*
vendedor-a; encargado-a de ventas	*salesman / woman*

6 El mundo del trabajo *Jobs and work*

Trabajo ...	*I work ...*
a tiempo parcial	*part-time*
como freelance	*freelance*
Soy autónomo-a.	*I am self-employed.*
Estoy desempleado-a/en paro.	*I am unemployed.*
el curso de reciclaje	*re-training course*
la oficina de empleo	*employment office*
el subsidio de desempleo	*unemployment benefit*

LOS SINDICATOS
UNIONS

el acuerdo	*agreement*
el/la afiliado-a	*trades union member*
la cuota de afiliado	*membership fee*
el/la delegado-a	*delegate*
el/la dirigente sindical	*trades union official*
el/la enlace sindical	*shop steward*
la huelga	*strike*
la huelga de celo	*work to rule*
la reunión sindical	*trades union meeting*
el sindicato	*trade union*
la tarjeta de afiliado; el carnet	*membership card*

EL SUELDO *PAY*

el día de paga	*pay day*
la hoja de sueldo; la nómina	*pay slip*
los ingresos; el sueldo	*earnings*
el impuesto sobre la renta	*income tax*
el IVA	*VAT*

el jornal	*wage*
el plan de pensiones	*pension plan*
las retenciones	*deductions*
la retención fiscal	*P.A.Y.E.*
el salario	*salary*
el seguro social	*National Insurance*
el sobre de paga	*pay packet*
la transferencia bancaria	*bank transfer*
semanal	*weekly*
mensual	*monthly*
neto	*net*
bruto	*gross*
asistir a una reunión	*to attend a meeting*
comprar	*to buy*
discutir	*to discuss*
(no) estar de acuerdo	*to agree / disagree*
ganar	*to earn*
fichar a la llegada/ a la salida	*to clock on / off*
hacer horas extraordinarias	*to do overtime*
tener reuniones	*to have meetings*

6 El mundo del trabajo *Jobs and work*

trabajar	*to work*	vender	*to sell*
trabajar por		viajar	*to travel*
turnos	*to work shifts*		

EL LUGAR DE TRABAJO *THE WORKPLACE*

Trabajo en . . .	*I work in a/an . . .*
El/ella trabaja en . . .	*He/she works in a/an*
un almacén	*warehouse*
un ambulatorio	*surgery*
una cadena de montaje	*assembly line*
casa	*at home*
una clínica	*clinic*
un colegio	*school*
el control de calidad	*quality control*
el embalaje	*packaging*
una empresa	*company*
un estudio	*studio*
una fábrica	*factory*
un hospital	*hospital*
un hotel	*hotel*
los negocios	*business*
una oficina	*office*
la oficina central	*head office*
la producción	*production*
un punto de venta al por menor	*retail outlet*
el reparto; la entrega	*delivery*
un restaurante	*restaurant*
el servicio de atención al cliente	*customer service*
una sociedad anónima (S.A.)	*limited company (Co. Ltd.)*
una sucursal	*subsidiary*
un supermercado	*supermarket*
un taller	*workshop*
una tienda	*shop*
las ventas al por mayor	*wholesale sales*
las ventas al por menor	*retail sales*

¡OTRA VEZ!

● *Activity: Write a list of five jobs. Can you say where they work?*

Por ejemplo:

mecánico – garaje
El mecánico trabaja en un garaje.

LA INDUSTRIA Y LAS EMPRESAS DE SERVICIOS
MANUFACTURING AND SERVICE INDUSTRIES

Trabajo en ...	*I work in ...*
Soy aprendiz-a en ...	*I am a trainee in ...*
una fábrica	*a factory*
el sector servicios	*the service industry*
la agricultura	*agriculture*
la banca	*banking*
la Bolsa	*the Stock Market*
el comercio	*commerce*
compras	*buying*
la confección	*clothing*
la construcción de carreteras	*road building*
diseño	*design*
una editorial	*publishing*
electrónica	*the electronics industry*
electrotécnica	*electrical engineering*
energía nuclear	*nuclear power*
la fabricación de herramientas	*tool making*
la horticultura	*horticulture*
hostelería	*catering*
la industria alimenticia	*food*
la industria del automóvil	*the motor industry*
la industria de la construcción	*the construction industry*
la industria del acero	*the steel industry*
la industria del carbón	*the coal industry*
la industria eléctrica	*the power industry*
la industria farmacéutica	*pharmaceutical industry*
la industria médica	*the medical industry*
informática	*computers / information technology*
la ingeniería civil	*civil engineering*
la investigación	*research*
maquinaria	*machinery*
ocio	*leisure*
periodismo	*the press; journalism*
seguros	*insurance*
telecomunicaciones	*telecommunications*
televisión	*television*
transporte	*transport*

6 El mundo del trabajo *Jobs and work*

transporte marítimo	*shipping*
ventas	*sales*
viajes y turismo	*travel and tourism*

Yo . . .	I . . .
ayudo (soy ayudante)	*assist*
coordino	*co-ordinate*
desarrollo	*develop*
diseño	*design*
escribo la correspondencia	*write letters*
fabrico	*manufacture*
hago demostraciones	*demonstrate*
hago el trabajo de oficina	*do the paperwork*
llevo la contabilidad	*do the accounts*
reparto; distribuyo	*distribute*
trabajo en publicidad	*write advertising*
vendo	*sell*

LA INDUSTRIA DE LA CONSTRUCCIÓN
THE CONSTRUCTION INDUSTRY

Los empleos *Jobs*

el albañil	*labourer; bricklayer*
el cantero	*stonemason*
el carpintero	*joiner*
el constructor	*builder*
el electricista	*electrician*
el escayolista	*plasterer*

el fontanero	*plumber*
el pintor decorador	*painter and decorator*
el técnico en calefacciones	*heating engineer*

Los materiales de construcción y las herramientas *Building materials and tools*

el aislamiento	*insulation*
el andamio	*scaffolding*
los azulejos	*wall tiles*
las baldosas	*floor tiles*
el cemento	*cement*
los cimientos	*foundations*
la construcción	*construction*
el cristal	*glass*
la cuerda	*string*
el doble acristalamiento	*double glazing*
la escalera	*ladder*
la escayola	*plaster*
la fibra de vidrio	*glass fibre*
la grava	*gravel*
la hormigonera	*cement mixer*
el ladrillo	*brick*
la madera	*wood*
la madera (de construcción)	*timber*
la medida	*measure*
la piedra	*stone*
la pizarra	*slates*
las tejas	*roof tiles*

6 El mundo del trabajo *Jobs and work*

La fontanería *Plumbing*

la calefacción	*heating*
las cañerías	*pipes*
el desagüe	*drain*
la ducha	*shower*
el grifo	*tap*
la llave de paso	*stopcock*
los radiadores	*radiators*
el revestimiento	*lagging*
el termo	*boiler*
el termostato	*thermostat*

La electricidad *Electrics*

los accesorios eléctricos	*light fittings*
los amperios	*amps*
la bombilla	*light bulb*
los cables	*wires*
el enchufe	*plug*
el fusible	*fuse*
el interruptor	*switch*
los voltios	*volts*

La pintura y la decoración *Painting and decorating*

el aguarrás	*turps*
el barniz	*varnish*
la brocha	*paint brush*
la escalera	*ladder*
la masilla	*filler*
el papel pintado	*wallpaper*
la pasta adhesiva	*paste*
la pintura	*paint*
la pintura esmalte	*gloss paint*
la pintura mate	*matt paint*
la pintura plástica	*plastic paint*
la pintura preparatoria	*undercoat*
la pulidora; la lijadora	*sander*
la quitapintura	*paint stripper*
el rodillo	*roller*
clavar	*to nail*
construir	*to build*
enyesar; enlucir	*to plaster*
excavar	*to excavate*
lijar	*to sand*
empapelar	*to paper*
martillar; golpear con martillo	*to hammer*
pintar	*to paint*
poner los cimientos	*to lay the foundations*
quitar; desprender	*to strip (wallpaper/paint)*
reparar	*to mend*

Las herramientas *Tools*

la caja de herramientas	*tool box*
el juego de herramientas	*tool kit*
la alargadera	*extension cable*
los alicates	*pliers*
el banco de trabajo	*workbench*
el cable	*cable*
el cepillo de carpintero	*plane*
el cincel	*chisel*
el clavo	*nail*
el destornillador	*screw driver*
el hacha	*axe*
la lijadora	*sander*

6 El mundo del trabajo *Jobs and work*

la llave (de tuercas)	*spanner*		el tornillo	*screw*
la llave inglesa	*monkey wrench*		la tuerca	*nut*
el martillo	*hammer*		atornillar	*to screw*
el mazo	*mallet*		clavar	*to hammer*
el perno	*bolt*		destornillar	*to unscrew*
el pico	*pick*		deshacer; aflojar	*to undo; loosen*
el taladro	*drill*		taladrar	*to drill*
el taladro eléctrico	*electric drill*			

LA SEGURIDAD EN EL TRABAJO
SAFETY AT WORK

Es obligatorio el uso del casco.
Helmets must be worn at all times.

el accidente	*accident*
el accidente laboral	*industrial accident*
la ambulancia	*ambulance*
la boca de incendios	*fire hydrant*
el bombero	*fireman*
la caída	*fall*
el coche de bomberos	*fire engine*
el cuerpo de bomberos	*fire brigade*
la descarga eléctrica	*electric shock*

Se prohibe (el uso de/el paso ...)	*Do not (use / enter ...)*
¡Peligro!	*Danger!*
¡Atención!	*Warning!*
¡No entrar!	*No entry!*
Prohibido fumar	*Smoking forbidden*
Se prohibe la entrada a toda persona ajena a la obra	*No admittance to unauthorised persons*
Salida	*Exit*
Salida de emergencia	*Emergency exit*
Salida de incendios	*Fire exit*
Punto de Reunión	*Assembly point*
Asistencia médica	*Medical assistance*
Botiquín	*Medical kit*

6 El mundo del trabajo *Jobs and work*

Rompa el cristal	*Break the glass*
Alarma	*Alarm*
Lávese las manos	*Wash your hands*
Usar ...	*Wear ...*
guantes	*gloves*
gafas	*goggles*
máscara	*a mask*
ropa	*sterilised*
esterilizada	*clothing*
ropa protectora	*protective clothing*

el extintor	*fire extinguisher*	caerse	*to fall*
el incendio	*fire*	cortarse	*to cut oneself*
los primeros		electrocutarse	*to be electrocuted*
auxilios	*first aid*	necesitar	*to need emergency*
la reanimación	*artificial*	tratamiento	*treatment*
artificial	*resuscitation*	de urgencia	
el seguro	*insurance*	sufrir un	
urgencias	*emergency services*	accidente	*to have an accident*

7 La empresa *The company*

la agencia	agency	el centro médico	medical centre
la empresa;		el depósito	store
la firma	firm	el establecimiento;	
la empresa		el local	premises
privada	private business	los obreros	shop floor
la fábrica	factory	las oficinas	offices
la franquicia	franchise	las oficinas de	
el servicio		plan abierto	open-plan
público	public utility	la recepción	reception
la sociedad		la sala de juntas	boardroom
anónima	limited company	el taller	workshop

EL PERSONAL
THE WORKFORCE

En la oficina *In the office*

la filial	subsidiary	el/la asesor-a	advisor
la oficina		el/la ayudante	assistant
central	head office	el/la ayudante	
la sucursal	branch	personal	personal assistant
		el/la consultor-a	consultant
las actividades de la		el/la director-a	
compañía	operations	comercial	commercial
el activo;			manager
el haber	assets	el/la director-a de	
el coche de		la compañía	company director
la empresa	company car	el/la director-a	
la conferencia;		financiero-a	financial director
el congreso	conference	el/la director-a	
el desarrollo	development	gerente	managing director
las directrices;		el/la interventor-a	
la política	company policy		credit controller
las ganancias/		la junta directiva	board of directors
las pérdidas	profit / loss	el/la secretario-a	company secretary
el informe	company report	el/la subdirector-a	deputy manager
el margen de		el/la vice-	
beneficios	profit margin	presidente-a	deputy chairman
la reunión	company meeting		
la transacción	deal	el/la agente	
		de seguros	insurance agent
comprar la		el/la archivero-a	filing clerk
parte de	to buy-out	el/la auditor-a	auditor
		el/la director-a	manager
el almacén	warehouse		
el aparcamiento	car park		
los aseos	washrooms		
la cantina	canteen		

7 La empresa *The company*

la gerencia intermedia	*middle management*
el guarda jurado	*security guard*
el/la jefe-a	*boss*
el/la limpiador-a	*cleaner*
el/la mecanó-grafo-a	*typist*
el/la mecanógrafo-a de dictáfono	*audio-typist*
el/la taquígrafo-a	*short-hand typist*
el/la mensajero-a	*courier*
el/la operador-a de centralita	*switchboard operator*
el/la recepcionista	*receptionist*
el/la representante	*representative*
el/la secretario-a	*secretary*
el/la supervisor-a	*office supervisor*
el/la viajante	*commercial traveller*
jubilado-a	*retired*
la pensión	*pension*
el/la pensionista	*pensioner*

Los obreros *The shop floor*

el/la aprendiz-a	*apprentice; trainee*
el capataz	*overseer; foreman*
el conserje	*caretaker*
el/la empleado-a	*employee*
el/la empleado-a a tiempo parcial	*part-time employee*
el empresario	*employer*
el/la obrero-a	*worker*
el peón	*labourer*
el/la responsable; jefe de grupo	*team leader*
el técnico	*technician*

Trabajo . . .	*I work . . .*
en turnos	*shifts*
a tiempo completo	*full time*
a tiempo parcial	*part-time*
con horario flexible	*flexitime*
Trabajo en el departamento de . . .	*I work in the . . . department*
administración	*administration*
compras	*buying / procurement*
contabilidad	*accounts*
control de calidad	*qualitity control*
exportación	*export*
fabricación	*manufacturing*
importación	*import*
mecanografía	*typing pool*
personal	*personnel*
publicidad	*publicity*
ventas/márketing	*sales / marketing*

7 La empresa *The company*

VENTAS, CONTABILIDAD Y ENVÍOS
SALES, ACCOUNTS AND DESPATCH

Ventas *Sales*

el análisis	*analysis*
el comerciante exclusivo	*sole agency, exclusivity*
el/la competidor-a	*competidor*
la compra	*purchase*
la concesión	*concession*
las condiciones de pago	*payment terms*
el/la consumidor-a	*consumer*
los contactos	*contacts*
el descuento	*discount*
el/la detallista; el/la comerciante al por menor	*retailer*
la distribución	*distribution*
la documentación	*documentation*
las exportaciones	*exports*
la garantía	*guarantee*
las importaciones	*imports*
libre de gastos de envío	*franco* (delivered 'free' with all duties paid)
el/la mayorista	*wholesaler*
el mercado nacional	*home market*
la muestra	*sample*
el negocio; el comercio	*business*
la oferta	*offer*
el ordenador	*computer*
la pieza	*component*
el pedido	*order*
el porcentaje	*percentage*
el presupuesto	*quotation*
la reclamación	*complaint*
el rendimiento	*performance*
la representación; la concesión	*dealership*
el tanto por ciento	*percent*
las ventas por correo	*mail order*
el viaje de negocios	*business journey*

Contabilidad *Accounts*

a crédito	*in credit*
el/la acreedor-a	*creditor*
el banco de compensación	*clearing bank*
la carta de crédito	*letter of credit*
el certificado de seguro	*insurance certificate*
el código bancario	*bank code*
el comprobante	*voucher*
las condiciones de crédito	*credit terms*
las condiciones de pago	*payment terms*
el coste	*cost*
el coste, seguro y flete	*CIF* (carriage, insurance and freight)
los costes fijos	*fixed costs*
el crédito	*credit*
la cuenta	*account*
el depósito	*deposit*
el/la deudor-a	*debtor*
el estado de cuenta	*statement*
el expediente	*file*
la expiración	*expiry*

7 La empresa *The company*

las facilidades crediticias	credit facilities
la factura	bill; invoice
la fecha límite	deadline
las finanzas	finance
franco fábrica	ex-works
franco; gratis; libre de gastos	free
el gasto; el desembolso	expenditure
los honorarios	fee
la indemnización	compensation
la liquidación	settlement
en metálico; en efectivo	cash
la nota de entrega	delivery note
el número de referencia	reference number
el organigrama	flow chart
el pago	payment
la pérdida	loss
la quiebra; la bancarrota	bankruptcy
el recibo	receipt
el reembolso; la devolución	refund
la referencia	reference
el saldo	balance

Envíos *Despatch*

las aduanas	customs
el/la agente expedidor	freight forwarder
el almacén	depot
los bienes; las mercancías	goods
la carga	freight (load)
el conocimiento de embarque	bill of lading
el contenedor	container

la demora	delay
disponible	available
no disponible	not available
el documento	document
en depósito	in storage
en existencias	in stock
fuera de existencias	out of stock
el envío	despatch
la entrega en fecha futura	forward delivery
el equipamiento	equipment
el excedente	excess
los gastos de transporte	transport costs
la letra de cambio	bill of exchange
la licencia	permit
las mercancías	freight (goods)
la red	network
pasado-a de fecha	out of date
el peso	weight
la remesa	consignment
el tamaño	size
el transbordo	transshipment
el tránsito; el paso	transit
el transporte	shipment
el transporte	transport
válido-a	valid

EL MÁRKETING Y LA PRODUCCIÓN *MARKETING AND PRODUCTION*

el análisis	research
el análisis de mercados	market research
el arancel	tariff

7 La empresa *The company*

las barreras arancelarias	*trade barriers*
la calidad	*quality*
la cámara de comercio	*chamber of commerce*
la campaña de ventas	*sales campaign*
la cantidad	*quantity*
el comercio	*trade; commerce*
la compra	*purchase*
las condiciones	*terms*
el contrato	*contract*
el control de calidad	*quality control*
la cuota	*quota*
los derechos de entrada	*import duty*
el director comercial	*marketing manager*
la distribución	*distribution*
el equipo; la maquinaria	*machinery*
el equipo de ventas	*sales team*
el excedente	*surplus*
la fabricación en serie	*mass production*
el/la fabricante	*manufacturer*
la gama de productos	*range of goods*
la gestión	*management*
el informe	*report*
el/la intérprete	*interpreter*
la licencia	*licence*
el líder del mercado	*market leader*
el logotipo	*logo*
la marca registrada	*trademark*
el márketing	*marketing*
las materias primas	*raw materials*
las negociaciones	*negotiations; talks*
el/la negociador-a	*negotiator*
el objetivo	*target*
la opción	*option*
el pago	*payment*
la planta; la fábrica	*plant*
el presupuesto	*estimate; budget*
la producción	*output*
el producto nacional bruto	*gross national product*
el programa	*schedule*
el progreso; la evolución	*progress*
la promoción	*promotion*
la promoción de ventas	*sales promotion*
el pronóstico de mercados	*market forecast*
el proyecto	*project*
la publicidad	*publicity*
el punto de venta	*point of sale*
la regulación	*regulation*
la renovación	*renewal*
la responsabilidad	*liability*
las restricciones arancelarias	*trade restrictions*
las tendencias de mercado	*market trends*
la transferencia	*transfer*
(a) largo plazo	*long term*
(a) corto plazo	*short term*
hecho-a a mano	*handmade*
oficial; autorizado-a	*official*

producido-a	
en serie	*mass produced*
el cartel	*poster*
el catálogo	*catalogue*
la exposición	*exhibition*
el/la expositor-a	*exhibitor*
la feria de	
muestras	*trade fair*
el folleto	*brochure*
la promoción	*promotion*
el stand	*stand*
administrar	*to manage*
comprar	*to buy*
dejar sin trabajo	*to make redundant*
despedir	*to sack*
dirigir	*to direct*
enviar	*to send*
exportar	*to export*
importar	*to import*
jubilarse	*to retire*
nombrar	*to appoint*
pagar	*to pay*
promover	*to promote*
repartir;	
entregar	*to deliver*
seleccionar;	
elegir	*to select*
transportar	*to transport*
vender	*to sell*

EN LA OFICINA
IN THE OFFICE

Material de oficina y mobiliario
Equipment

el archivador	*filing cabinet*
el bolígrafo	*pen; biro*
el borrador;	
la goma	*rubber; eraser*

el cajón	*drawer*
la calculadora	*calculator*
el calendario	*calendar*
la chincheta	*drawing pin*
la cinta	
adhesiva	*sticky tape*
el clip	*paper clip*
el diccionario	*dictionary*
el dictáfono	*dictating machine*
la entrada/salida de	
documentos	*in-/out-tray*
el escritorio	*desk*
las etiquetas	
adhesivas	*sticky labels*
el expediente	*file*
el fax	*fax machine*
la fotocopiadora	*photocopier*
la franqueadora	*franking machine*
la grapadora	*stapler*
las grapas	*staples*
la impresora	*printer*
el lápiz	*pencil*
la máquina	
de café	*coffee machine*
la máquina	
de escribir	*typewriter*
la mesa	*table*
el ordenador	*computer*
el papel	*paper*
el papel cello	*sellotape*
la papelera	*waste bin*
el pegamento	*glue*
la regla	*ruler*
los sellos	*stamps*
la silla giratoria	*swivel chair*
el sobre	*envelope*
la taladradora	*hole punch*
el teléfono	*telephone*
las tijeras	*scissors*
la trituradora	*shredder*
el ventilador	*ventilator*

7 La empresa *The company*

¿Puedo hacer una fotocopia?	*Can I make a photo copy?*
¿Puedo usar el fax?	*Can I use the fax machine?*
Correr/descorrer las cortinas	*Draw the blinds / curtains*
Abrir/cerrar la ventana	*Open / close the window*

El ordenador *The computer*

la base de datos	*database*
el camino	*path*
el CD ROM	*CD-ROM*
la cinta	*tape*
el correo electrónico	*electronic mail*
el cursor	*cursor*
el disco duro	*hard disk*
el disquete	*disquette*
el escáner	*scanner*
la hoja de cálculo	*spreadsheet*
el icono	*icon*
la impresora	*printer*
la instalación	*installation*
el interruptor	*switch*
el lector	*drive*
el lector CD-ROM	*CD-ROM drive*
la memoria	*memory*
la memoria RAM	*RAM*
la memoria ROM	*ROM*
el menú	*menu*
el módem	*modem*
el monitor	*monitor*
el multimedia	*multimedia*
la pantalla	*screen*
el procesador de textos	*word processor*
el procesamiento de textos	*word processing*
el programa	*programme*
el ratón	*mouse*
la tecla	*key*
el teclado	*keyboard*
la terminal	*terminal*
la ventana	*window*
el virador	*toner*
el virus	*virus*

No funciona. ¿Cómo se . . . ?	*It doesn't work. How do you . . . ?*
apaga	*switch off*
enciende	*switch on*
entra	*enter*
entra en el programa	*get into the programme*
guarda	*save*
hace back up	*back-up*
hace clic	*click*
pulsa	*press*
instala	*instal*
subraya	*underline*
teclea	*key in*
vuelve a rellenar	*re-fill*

¡OTRA VEZ!

● *Activity:* Diga los nombres de los objetos en esta oficina. *Label the objects in this office.*

EL TELÉFONO
THE TELEPHONE

la centralita	*switchboard*
el contestador automático	*answering machine*
la extensión	*extension*
la guía telefónica	*telephone directory*
el localizador personal; el busca	*pager*
el módem	*modem*
el teléfono	*phone*
el teléfono móvil	*mobile phone*
el teléfono analógico	*analogue phone*
el teléfono digital	*digital phone*
el teléfono móvil del coche	*car phone*
el fax	*fax*
la información	*directory enquiries*
la llamada a cobro revertido	*reverse charge call*
el mensaje; el recado	*message*
el número de teléfono	*phone number*
el prefijo	*dialling code*
el tono de marcar	*dialling tone*
(estar) comunicando	*engaged*
no funciona	*out of order*

AL TELÉFONO *ON THE PHONE*

¡Diga!	*Hello!*
¿En qué puedo ayudarle?	*Can I help you?*
¿Puedo hablar con . . .?	*Can I speak to . . .?*
¿Puede ponerme con la extensión . . .?	*Can I have extension . . .?*
¡Un momento!	*Hold on!*
El/ella no está	*He / she is not there.*
El/ella está hablando.	*He / she is on the other line.*
¿Puede llamarme luego?	*Can he / she / you call back later?*
¿Puedo coger/dejar un mensaje?	*Can I take / leave a message?*
Gracias por su llamada.	*Thank you for calling.*
De nada.	*Don't mention it.*
Lo siento, me he confundido de número.	*I'm sorry, I've got the wrong number.*
¿Cómo se escribe?	*Can you spell it?*
¿Puede repetir?	*Can you repeat it?*
¿Puede hablar más despacio?	*Can you speak more slowly?*
Deje su mensaje después de la señal.	*Leave a message after the tone.*
Llame después de . . .	*Ring after . . .*
Es urgente.	*It's urgent.*

llamar	*to call*	telefonear	*to phone*
mandar un fax	*to send a fax*	volver a llamar	*to call back*

CITAS Y EXCUSAS
ARRANGING MEETINGS AND MAKING EXCUSES

¿Dónde nos vemos?	*Where shall we meet?*
Nos vemos . . .	*Let's meet . . .*
en el aparcamiento	*in the car park*
en el bar	*in the bar*
en el campo de golf	*on the golf course*
en mi casa	*at my house*
en el cruce de . . .	*at the junction of . . .*
en frente de la estación	*opposite the station*
en la estación	*at the station*
en el hotel	*in the hotel*

7 La empresa *The company*

en mi/tu oficina	*in my / your office*
en recepción	*at reception*
en el restaurante	*at the restaurant*
en el vestíbulo	*in the foyer*

Yo te recogeré.	*I'll pick you up.*	No tengo tiempo.	*I haven't the time.*
¿Cuándo nos vemos?	*When shall we meet?*	Tengo demasiado trabajo.	*I have too much work.*
a las diez	*at 10 o'clock*	No me interesa.	*I'm not interested.*
dentro de media hora	*in half an hour*	Tengo una cita/un compromiso.	*I have an appointment.*
dentro de cinco minutos	*in five minutes*	Estoy ocupado-a	*I'm busy.*
mañana	*tomorrow*		
		Tengo que ir . . .	*I have to go to . . .*
Lo siento.	*I'm sorry.*	al dentista	*the dentist*
No quiero.	*I don't want to.*	al médico	*the doctor*
No puedo.	*I can't.*	al hospital	*the hospital*

¡OTRA VEZ!

● *Activity:* Lo siento, no puedo . . . *I'm sorry, I can't make it, I . . .*

8 El arte y los medios de comunicación *Art and the media*

EL ARTE Y LOS ARTISTAS
ART AND ARTISTS

El arte *Art*

el/la artista	*artist*
la colección	*art collection*
el/la diseñador-a	*designer*
la exposición	*art exhibition*
el/la grafista	*graphic artist*
el/la ilustrador-a	*illustrator*
el museo de bellas artes	*art gallery*

El dibujo y la pintura
Drawing and painting

la acuarela	*water colour*
el apunte	*sketch*
el bodegón	*still life*
el caballete	*easel*
el carboncillo	*charcoal*
el cuadro	*picture*
el dibujo	*drawing*
el lápiz	*crayon*
el lienzo	*canvas*
el marco	*picture frame*
el óleo	*oil painting*
el paisaje	*landscape*
el pastel	*pastels*
el pincel	*paint brush*
la pintura	*painting*
las pinturas	*paints*
el retrato	*portrait*

La cerámica y la escultura
Pottery and sculpture

el/la alfarero-a; el/la ceramista	*potter*
la alfarería; la cerámica	*pottery*

el barniz	*varnish*
el barro	*clay*
la maceta/ el tiesto	*pot*
el torno	*wheel*

el/la escultor-a	*sculptor*
la escultura	*sculpture*
el busto	*bust*
el cincel	*chisel*
el estudio; el taller	*studio*
el/la modelo	*model*
la talla	*carving*
el vaciado	*cast*
la artesanía	*craftmanship*
el/la artesano-a	*craftsman*

La arquitectura *Architecture*

el/la arquitecto	*architect*
el edificio	*building*
los planos	*plans*
barroco	*Baroque*
clásico	*Classic*
gótico	*Gothic*
mudéjar	*Mudejar* (Arab style under Catholic rule)
plateresco	*Plateresque*
románico	*Roman*
cocer	*to fire*
colorear	*to colour*
dibujar	*to draw*
diseñar	*to design*
esculpir	*to sculpt*
exponer	*to exhibit*
hacer un boceto	*to sketch*
pintar	*to paint*
tallar	*to carve*
tornear	*to throw*

8 El arte y los medios de comunicación *Art and the media*

LA PALABRA ESCRITA: LOS LIBROS, LAS REVISTAS, LOS PERIÓDICOS
THE WRITTEN WORD: BOOKS, MAGAZINES, NEWSPAPERS

el/la articulista; cronista	*feature writer*
el/la autor-a	*author*
el/la biógrafo-a	*biographer*
la casa editorial	*publisher*
el/la diseñador-a	*designer*
el/la diseñador-a gráfico	*graphic designer*
el/la fotógrafo-a	*photographer*
el/la historiador-a	*historian*
el/la novelista	*novelist*
el/la periodista	*journalist*
el/la poeta	*poet*

los derechos de autor	*royalties; copyright*
la escritura	*hand writing*
la máquina de escribir	*typewriter*
el procesador de textos	*word processor*

el cómic	*comic*
el libro	*book*
el periódico; el diario	*newspaper*
la revista	*magazine*

diario	*daily*
semanal	*weekly*
quincenal	*bi-weekly*
mensual	*monthly*

la autobiografía	*autobiography*
la biografía	*biography*
la ciencia ficción	*science fiction*
el diccionario	*dictionary*
el documento	*document*
la enciclopedia	*encyclopaedia*
el folleto	*brochure*
el libro/la edición de bolsillo	*pocket book*
el libro de frases	*phrase book*
el libro de referencia	*reference book*
el libro de texto	*text book*
el libro de viajes	*travel book*
la novela de suspense; de misterio	*thriller*
la novela negra	*crime story*
el relato; el cuento	*short story*
el relato de detectives	*detective story*

el artículo	*article*
el bolígrafo	*pen*
el capítulo	*chapter*
la carta	*letter (correspondence)*
el cuento; la historia	*story*
el cuento de hadas	*fairy tale*
el ejemplar	*volume*
el/la escritor-a	*writer*
la ficción	*fiction*
la frase; la oración	*sentence*
la frase; la expresión	*phrase*
la guía	*guide book*
el horóscopo	*horoscope*
la idea general	*outline*
el índice	*index*
el índice de materias	*contents*

la lámina;	
la ilustración	*illustration*
la letra	*letter* (of alphabet)
la leyenda	*legend*
la línea	*line*
el manual	*manual*
el libro de	
consulta	*handbook*
la novela	*novel*
la novela	
histórica	*historical novel*
la obra de teatro	*play*
la página	*page*
la palabra	*word*
el papel	*paper*
el párrafo	*paragraph*
la pluma	*fountain pen*
el poema	*poem*
la poesía	*poetry*
la portada	*cover*
la cubierta	*hard cover*
el libro	
de bolsillo	*paper back*
el prospecto	*leaflet*
el serial;	
la novela por	
entregas	*serial*
la tinta	*ink*

La prensa *Newspapers*

los anuncios	*advertisements*
los anuncios	
por palabras	*small ads.*
el artículo	*article*
la Bolsa	*stock market report*
las cartas al	
director	*letters to the editor*
la cartelera	*what's on*
la composición	*layout*
el consultorio	*problem page*
el crucigrama	*crossword*
la cultura	*arts*

los deportes	*sport*
la economía	*financial news*
el editorial; el artículo	
de fondo	*editorial*
las farmacias	*emergency*
de guardia	*chemists*
el humor	*cartoons*
el jeroglífico	*puzzles*
las necrológicas	*obituaries*
la política	*politics*
la primera	
plana	*front page*
la revista	*reviews*
sociedad	*social*
el suplemento	*supplement*
los teléfonos de	*emergency*
urgencia	*telephone numbers*
la televisión/	
radio	*television / radio*
el tiempo	*weather report*
los titulares	*headlines*
los toros; la lidia	*bullfight reports*
regional	*local news*
nacional	*national news*
internacional	*international news*

La opinión *Opinion*

el cuestionario	*questionnaire*
la desventaja	*disadvantage*
la diferencia	*difference*
la encuesta	*survey*
la semejanza	*similarity*
la ventaja	*advantage*
brevemente	*in short*
creer	*to believe*
depende de	*it depends*
de todas formas	*all the same*
extraordinario-a	*extraordinary*
habitual; corriente	*usual*
para terminar	*in conclusion*

pensar	*to think*	corregir	*to correct*
poco habitual;		corregir las	
poco corriente	*unusual*	pruebas	*to proof read*
por otra parte	*on the other hand*	escribir	*to write*
por último	*finally*	escribir a	
por una parte	*on the one hand*	máquina	*to type*
se trata de	*it's a question of;*	imprimir	*to print*
	it's about	leer	*to read*
sin comentarios	*no comment*	preparar para	
según los sondeos		la imprenta	*to edit*
de opinión	*according to the polls*	publicar por	
		entregas	*to serialise*
dudar	*to doubt*	puntuar	*to punctuate*
estar		sangrar	*to indent*
equivocado	*to be wrong*	usar	
preferir	*to prefer*	mayúsculas	*to use capital letters*
ser necesario	*to be necessary*	usar minúsculas	*to use small letters*
tener razón	*to be right*		

el acento	*accent (´)*
la diéresis	*diaeresis (¨)*
la tilde	*tilde (~)*

EL CINE Y EL TEATRO
CINEMA AND THEATRE

la coma	*comma*
las comillas	*inverted commas*
los dos puntos	*colon*
el guión	*hyphen*
el paréntesis	*brackets*
el punto	*full stop*
el punto y coma	*semi-colon*
el signo de	
admiración	*exclamation mark*
el signo de	
interrogación	*question mark*
el tipo de letra	*font*

El cine *The cinema*

la banda sonora	*sound track*
el cine	*cinema*
la entrada	*ticket*
la fila	*row*
la localidad;	
la butaca	*seat*
la pantalla	*screen*
el pase	*performance*
el pasillo	*aisle*
la película;	
el filme	*film*
el público	*audience*
la taquilla	*ticket office*
el vestíbulo	*foyer*

cursiva	*italic*
negrita	*bold*

Los géneros de las películas *Film types*

la película ...	... (film)
de amor	*love story*
de ciencia ficción	*science fiction*
de detectives	*detective*
de guerra	*war*
de miedo	*horror film*
de suspense	*thriller*
del espacio	*space*
del oeste	*western*
pornográfica	*pornographic*
romántica	*romance*
violenta	*violent*

censurada	*censored*
cortada	*cut*
doblada	*dubbed*
muda	*silent*
subtitulada	*sub-titled*
una comedia	*comedy*
en versión original	*original version (subtitled)*
no aconsejada para menores de ...	*Not suitable for people under ... years*

el actor/la actriz	*actor / actress*
el/la ayudante de producción	*assistant producer*
el cámara	*cameraman*
el/la director-a	*director*
el/la estrella de cine	*film star*
el/la productor-a	*producer*
el/la técnico de sonido	*sound technician*
trataba de ...	*It was about ...*

Era una película ...	*It was a ... film*
buena	*good*
emocionante	*exciting*
mala	*bad*
horrible	*awful*
aburrida	*boring*
Estaba bien/mal rodada.	*It was well / badly filmed.*
(No) la recomendaría.	*I would (not) recommend it.*
Quisiera dos entradas para ...	*I would like two tickets for ...*
No hay entradas; localidades	*It's sold out.*
Quisiera reservar ...	*I would like to book ...*

8 El arte y los medios de comunicación *Art and the media*

El teatro *The theatre*

el anfiteatro	*circle*
el auditorio	*auditorium*
los bastidores	*wings*
las butacas	*stalls*
las candilejas	*footlights*
el decorado	*scenery*
el escenario	*stage*
el guardarropa	*cloakroom*
las luces	*lights*
el paraíso	*balcony*
el palco	*box*
la salida	*exit*
la salida de emergencia	*emergency exit*
el telón	*curtain*
la tribuna	*gallery*

La obra *The play*

el actor	*actor*
la actriz	*actress*
los aplausos	*applause*
el argumento; la trama	*plot*
el/la crítico-a	*critic*
los decorados	*set*
el entreacto; el intermedio	*interval*
la escena	*scene*
la función	*show*
la función de tarde	*matinee*
el maquillaje	*make-up*
el miedo al público	*stage fright*
el nerviosismo	*nerves*
la noche del estreno	*first-night*
el papel	*part; role*
el personaje	*character*
el primer acto	*act 1*

la producción	*production*
el programa	*programme*
la reseña	*review*
el traje	*costume*

La ópera *Opera*

el coro	*chorus*
el/la director-a (de orquesta)	*conductor*
la orquesta	*orchestra*
el reparto	*cast*
el/la solista	*soloist*

El ballet *Ballet*

el/la bailarín-a	*ballet dancer*
el coreógrafo	*choreographer*
el cuerpo de ballet	*corps de ballet*
la prima ballerina	*prima ballerina*

El drama *Drama*

el/la apuntador-a	*prompt (-er)*
el/la director-a de escena	*stage manager*
el escenógrafo	*designer*
el/la primera figura	*star*
el/la productor-a	*producer*
el/la suplente	*understudy*

El circo *Circus*

el/la acróbata	*acrobat*
los animales amaestrados	*performing animals*
el/la artista	*artist*
la carpa	*big top*

el payaso	*clown*
la pista	*ring*
el/la trapecista	*trapeze artist*
la comedia	*comedy*
el drama histórico	*historical drama*
la farsa	*farce*
el musical	*musical*
la revista	*review*
los títeres	*puppet show*
actuar	*to perform*
bailar	*to dance*
hacer el papel de	*to play the role of*
representar	*to act*
tomar la delantera	*to take the lead*
abuchear	*to boo*
aplaudir	*to clap*
disfrutar/pasarlo bien	*to enjoy*
mirar	*to watch*
(no) gustar	*(not) to like*

La música *Music*

el/la cantante	*singer*
el/la intérprete	*player*
los instrumentos	*instruments*
el músico	*musician*

La música pop *Pop music*

el acorde	*chord*
las altavoces	*loudspeakers*
los amplificadores	*amplifiers*
el bajo	*bass guitar*
el batería	*drummer*
la batería	*drums*
el conjunto	*band*
los 40 principales	*Top 40*
el disc jockey; el pinchadiscos	*disc jockey*
el empresario; el agente	*impresario*
la estrella de pop	*pop star*
un éxito musical	*hit*
el grupo	*group*
la guitarra	*guitar*
el/la guitarrista	*guitarist*
la melodía	*tune*
el teclado	*keyboard*
el rock	*rock*
el pop	*pop*
el country and western	*country and western*
el folk	*folk*
el jazz	*jazz*
el flamenco	*flamenco*

La música clásica *Classical music*

el/la acompañante	*accompanist*
el/la cantante	*singer*
el/la compositor-a	*composer*
el coro	*choir*
la orquesta	*orchestra*
la partitura	*score*
el/la pianista	*pianist*
barítono	*bass*
contralto	*alto*
soprano	*soprano*
tiple	*treble*

Los instrumentos *Instruments*

Los instrumentos
  de cuerda   **Strings**
el arpa   *harp*
el banjo   *banjo*
el contrabajo   *double bass*
la guitarra   *guitar*
la viola   *viola*
el violín   *violin*
el violoncelo   *cello*

Los instrumentos
  de aire   **Wind**
                       instruments
el clarinete   *clarinet*
la flauta   *flute*
el oboe   *oboe*
el saxofón   *saxophone*
el trombón   *trombone*
la trompa   *horn*
la trompeta   *trumpet*
la tuba   *tuba*

Los instrumentos
  de percusión   **Percussion**
las castañuelas   *castanets*
la pandereta   *tamborine*
el tambor   *drum*
el tamboril   *side drum*
el timbal   *kettle drum*
el triángulo   *triangle*

el clavicordio   *harpsichord*
el órgano   *organ*
el piano   *piano*

el/la primer
  violín   *leader*
el/la solista   *soloist*
el solo   *solo*
el dúo   *duet*
la orquesta de
  cámara   *chamber orchestra*

el cassette   *cassette recorder*
el CD   *CD*
la cinta   *cassette*
el disco   *record*
el lector de CD   *CD player*
el micrófono   *microphone*
el tocadiscos   *record player*

La escala *The scale*

el tono   *key*
desafinado   *flat*
agudo/sostenido   *sharp*
mayor   *major*
menor   *minor*
afinado   *in tune*
tener oído   *to have*
  perfecto   *perfect pitch*

un/una
  buen-a/mal-a   *a good / poor*
  músico-a   *musician*
una buena/
  mala voz   *a good / poor voice*

afinar   *to tune*
cantar   *to sing*
grabar   *to record; tape*
rasguear   *to strum*
tocar   *to play*

LA RADIO Y LA TELEVISIÓN
RADIO AND TELEVISION

la televisión/TV	*TV*
la radio	*radio*
la antena	*aerial*
la audiencia	*audience*
la cadena	*channel*
el cámara	*cameraman*
la cámara de vídeo	*video camera*
el corresponsal	*correspondant*
el/la editor-a	*editor*
la entrevista	*interview*
la grabación	*recording*
el ingeniero de sonido	*sound engineer*
la interferencia	*interference*
el mando a distancia	*remote control*
las noticias; el informativo	*news broadcast*
el/la oyente	*listener*
el/la presentador-a	*presenter*
el/la productor-a	*producer*
el programa en directo	*live programme*
los rótulos	*credits*
el/la televidente	*viewer*
la televisión por cable	*cable TV*
la televisión por satélite	*satellite TV*

el vídeo	*video recorder*
los anuncios	*commercials*
la comedia	*comedy*
el concurso	*games show*
los dibujos animados	*cartoon*
el documental	*documentary*
el programa	*programme*
el programa de viajes	*travel show*
el reality show	*tabloid TV show*
la retransmisión	*repeat*
la telenovela	*soap*
el programa de entrevistas/ la tertulia	*chat show*
apagar	*to switch off*
averiarse	*to break down*
borrar	*to wipe off*
cambiar de cadena	*to change channels*
encender	*to switch on*
grabar	*to record*
poner	*to play back*
sintonizar	*to tune*
¿Viste ... ?	*Did you see ... ?*
¿Has visto ... ?	*Have you seen ... ?*
¿Qué te pareció ... ?	*What did you think of ... ?*

EL OCIO
LEISURE

Los lugares de reunión
Venues

el bar	*bar*
el bingo	*bingo hall*
la bolera	*bowling alley*
el casino	*casino*
el circo	*circus*
el club	*club*
el club juvenil	*youth club*
la discoteca	*disco*

el estadio	*stadium*
la feria de atracciones	*fun fair*
la fiesta	*party*
el hipódromo	*race course*
el night club	*night club*
el parque	*park*
el parque temático	*theme park*
la piscina	*swimming pool*
la pista de hielo	*ice rink*
la sala de conciertos	*concert hall*

Me gusta(-n) . . .	*I like . . .*
las actividades al aire libre	*outdoor pursuits*
bailar	*dancing*
coleccionar	*collecting*
sellos	*stamps*
postales	*postcards*
reproducciones de . . .	*model . . .*
coser	*sewing*
dibujar	*drawing*
escuchar música	*listening to music*
hacer footing	*jogging*
hacer punto	*knitting*
leer	*reading*
montar a caballo	*horse riding*
montar en bicicleta	*cycling*
nadar	*swimming*
pasear	*walking*
pescar	*fishing*
pintar	*painting*
tocar un instrumento musical	*playing music*
el bricolaje	*D.I.Y*
la fotografía	*photography*
la jardinería	*gardening*
el senderismo	*hiking*

Salir *Going out*

Me gusta ir . . .	*I like going to . . .*
al cine	*the cinema*
a la discoteca	*discos*
a una fiesta	*parties*
a un polideportivo	*the sports centre*
al restaurante	*restaurants*
al teatro	*the theatre*

Me gusta (jugar al tenis).	*I like (playing tennis).*
Me gustaría (jugar al tenis).	*I would like (to play tennis).*
Prefiero (salir a tomar una copa).	*I prefer (to go for a drink).*
No me gusta (jugar al tenis).	*I don't like (playing tennis).*
Odio (jugar al tenis).	*I hate (playing tennis).*

LOS PASATIEMPOS
HOBBIES

Las cartas, el ajedrez y los juegos de mesa
Cards, chess and board games

el ajedrez	*chess*
el juego de cartas	*card game*
el juego de mesa	*board game*

Las cartas *Cards*

la baraja de cartas	*pack of cards*
el palo	*suit*
los corazones	*hearts*
los diamantes	*diamonds*
las picas	*spades*
los tréboles	*clubs*
el as	*ace*
el comodín	*joker*

la reina; la dama	*queen*
el rey	*king*
la sota	*jack*
el triunfo	*trump*
el bridge	*bridge*
la canasta	*canasta*
el póker	*poker*
el whist	*whist*
el mus	*popular Spanish card game*
el/la jugador-a	*player*
jugar	*to play*
Te toca a ti.	*It's your turn.*

El ajedrez *Chess*

el alfil	*bishop*
el caballo	*knight*
el peón	*pawn*
la reina	*queen*
el rey	*king*
la torre	*castle / rook*

9 El ocio y los deportes *Hobbies and sports*

blanco	*white*
negro	*black*
jaque	*check*
jaque mate	*checkmate*
mover	*to move*
Te toca mover a ti.	*It's your move.*
enrocar	*to castle*
¡jaque!	*check!*
¡jaque mate!	*check mate!*
¡No puedes hacer eso!	*You can't do that!*
Tienes que . . .	*You have to . . .*

Otros juegos *Other games*

los dados	*dice*
las damas	*draughts*
el dominó	*dominoes*
la oca	*Spanish 'snakes and ladders'*
el parchís	*parcheesi*
la casilla	*'square'*
la pieza	*'man'*
el reloj automático	*timer*
el tablero	*board*
la lotería	*lottery*
el cupón (de los ciegos)	*lottery ticket (for ONCE-association for the blind)*
el décimo	*lottery ticket*
el gordo	*jackpot*
el número del décimo	*lottery number*
el número premiado	*winning number*
el premio	*lottery prize*
la quiniela	*football pools*
el sorteo	*draw*

BAILAR DANCING

el baile disco	*disco*
el baile folklórico	*folk / country dancing*
el baile swing	*jive*
el merengue	*merengue*
la salsa	*salsa*
el tango	*tango*
el vals	*waltz*
la sala de baile	*ballroom*

Bailes folklóricos españoles *Spanish folk dances*

el flamenco	*(Andalucía)*
la jota	*(Aragón/La Mancha)*
la muñeira	*(Galicia)*
las sevillanas	*(Andalucía)*
la sardana	*(Cataluña)*
el compás	*beat*
la pareja	*partner*
el paso	*step*
el ritmo	*rhythm*

LA PESCA FISHING

el agua salada	*salt water*
el agua dulce	*fresh water*
la pesca (con caña)	*angling*
la pesca (con mosca)	*fly fishing*
la pesca de agua dulce	*coarse fishing*
el pez – los peces	*fish*
el anzuelo	*hook*
la barca	*boat*
las botas altas de goma	*waders*

la caña	rod
el cebo	bait
la cesta	basket
la cuchara	landing net
la mosca seca	dry fly
la mosca	fly
el peso	weight
la red	net
los remos	oars
el sedal	line
la silla de tijera	stool

Los peces de agua dulce
Freshwater fish

la perca	perch
el salmón	salmon
la trucha	trout

Los peces de mar Sea fish

el arenque	herring
el atún	tuna
el bacalao	cod
la caballa	mackerel
los calamares	squid
el cazón	dogfish
el choco	cuttlefish
la merluza	hake
la pescadilla	whiting
el pez espada	swordfish
el pulpo	octopus
el rape	angler fish
la sardina	sardine
el tiburón	shark

Los mariscos Shellfish

las almejas	clams
los berberechos	cockles
el camarón	shrimp
el cangrejo	crab

la cigala	Dublin bay prawn (scampi)
la gamba	prawn
la langosta	lobster
el langostino	large prawn
los mejillones	mussels
las vieiras	scallops
pescar	to fish
capturar	to catch

LA EQUITACIÓN
HORSES AND RIDING

el caballo	horse
el poney	pony
el semental	stallion
la yegua	mare
los arneses	harness
la brida	bridle
la cuadra	stable
el estribo	stirrup
la explanada de ensillado; el paddock	paddock
el salto	jump
la silla de montar	saddle
las botas de montar	riding boots
la chaqueta de montar	riding coat
la fusta	crop
la gorra de montar	riding hat
los pantalones de montar	jodhpurs
apostar	to bet
la apuesta	bet
las carreras de caballos	horse racing

la carrera de caballos			la composición	setting
sin obstáculos	flat race		la copia	copy; print
el corredor			el cuarto oscuro	dark room
de apuestas	bookie		la diapositiva	slide
el/la ganador-a	winner		la exposición	
el hipódromo	race course		insuficiente	under exposure
el jockey	jockey		el exposímetro	exposure meter
			el flash	flash
caerse	to fall off		el/la fotógrafo	photographer
cuidar los			el fotómetro	light meter
caballos	to groom		granangular	wide angle
ganar	to win		la máquina	
ir al trote	to trot		(fotográfica)	camera
montar a caballo	to ride		mate/brillo	matt / glossy
			el negativo	negative

LA FOTOGRAFÍA
PHOTOGRAPHY

			el objetivo	lens
la abertura	aperture		la película	
el álbum	album		rápida/lenta	fast / slow film
la ampliación	enlargement		la pila	battery
automático-a	automatic		la tapa del	
en blanco			objetivo	lens cap
y negro	black and white		el teleobjetivo	telephoto lens
la bombilla			el tiempo de	exposure time
de flash	flash bulb		revelado	(developing)
en color	colour		el trípode	tripod
			el visor	view finder

El rebobinador/el flash no funciona.	The winder / flash doesn't work.

ampliar	to enlarge		rebobinar	to re-wind
enfocar	to focus		revelar	to develop
exponer	to expose		sacar una foto	to take a photo
hacer copias	to print			

9 El ocio y los deportes *Hobbies and sports*

LOS DEPORTES – GENERAL
SPORTS – GENERAL

el auto-movilismo	*motor racing*
el balonmano	*handball*
el billar	*billiards; pool*
el juego de bolos	*skittles*
la lucha libre	*wrestling*
el monopatín	*skate boarding*
el motociclismo	*motorcycle racing*
el patinaje sobre ruedas	*roller skating*
el rugby	*rugby*
el squash	*squash*
el voleibol	*volleyball*

Las artes marciales
Martial arts

el judo	*judo*
el tae kwando	*tae kwando*
el cinturón	*belt*
el traje	*suit*

El bádminton *Badminton*

la raqueta	*racquet*
la red	*net*
el volante	*shuttlecock*
la pista	*court*

El baloncesto *Basketball*

el cesto	*basket*

Los bolos *Bowls*

el boliche	*jack*

El boxeo *Boxing*

el asalto	*round*
los guantes de boxeo	*gloves*
el K.O.	*knockout*
el ring	*ring*

Los dardos *Darts*

el blanco	*dart board*
el dardo	*dart*

El entrenamiento
Fitness training

el aerobic	*aerobics*
la bicicleta estática	*exercise bike*
el footing; el jogging	*jogging*
las pesas	*weights*

La esgrima *Fencing*

la careta	*mask*
el florete	*foil*

La gimnasia *Gymnastics*

la cama elástica	*trampoline*
la colchoneta	*mat*
las paralelas	*parallel bars*
el potro	*horse*
el suelo	*floor*

El hockey *Hockey*

el palo	*stick*
la portería	*goal*

El snooker *Snooker*

la bola	*ball*
la mesa	*table*
el taco	*cue*

9 El ocio y los deportes *Hobbies and sports*

El tenis de mesa; el pingpong
Table tennis

la mesa	*table*
la pala	*bat*

El tiro *Shooting*

la bala	*bullet*
el campo de tiro	*rifle range*
la munición	*ammunition*
el rifle	*rifle*
el tiro al plato/ de pichón	*clay pigeon shooting*

El tiro al arco *Archery*

el arco	*bow*
el blanco; la diana	*target*
la flecha	*arrow*

Los deportes aeronáuticos
Air sports

el ala delta	*hang gliding*
la aviación	*flying*
el paracaidismo	*parachuting*
el planeo	*gliding*
volar en globo	*ballooning*

Los deportes de montaña
Mountain sports

la escalada en rocas	*rock climbing*
el excursionismo a pie	*mountain walking/ hiking*
el montañismo	*mountain climbing*
la orientación	*orienteering*
los arreos	*harness*

las botas de escalar	*climbing boots*
las clavijas de escala	*pitons*
la cuerda	*rope*
la mochila	*rucksack*
la piqueta	*ice axe*
la ropa térmica	*thermal clothing*
la ruta; el itinerario	*route*
el saco de dormir	*sleeping bag*
la tienda	*tent*

El fútbol *Football*

el campo	*pitch*
el club	*club*
el equipo	*team*
el partido	*match*
el árbitro	*referee*
el capitán	*captain*
el encargado de campo	*groundsman*
el entrenador	*trainer*
el/la espectador-a	*spectator*
el juez de línea	*linesman*
el jugador	*player*
la liga	*league*
la copa	*cup*
la línea	*line*
el poste de la portería	*goal post*
fuera de juego	*off-side*
fuera de línea	*over the line*
los puestos	*positions*
el ataque	*attack*
el defensa	*back / defence*

9 El ocio y los deportes *Hobbies and sports*

el delantero	*forward*	la dejada	*let*
el medio	*centre*	el servicio	*service*
el portero	*goalkeeper*		
		cero	*love*
ganar	*to win*	quince iguales	*15 all*
empatar	*to draw*	ventaja	*advantage*
perder	*to lose*	cuarenta iguales	*deuce*
		el tiebreak	*tiebreak*
chutar	*to shoot*	juego, set	
dar un puntapié	*to kick*	y partido	*game, set and match*
fallar	*to miss*		
marcar (un gol)	*to score (a goal)*		
		servir	*to serve*
el cabezazo	*header*	jugar	*to play*
el penalti	*penalty*	volear	*to volley*

El equipamiento protector
Protective equipment

El golf *Golf*

la bandera	*flag*
el bunker	*bunker*

la codera	*elbow guard*
la rodillera	*knee guard*

el cadi	*caddie*
el campo de golf	*golf course*
el club de golf	*golf club*

El tenis *Tennis*

el fairway; la calle	*fairway*
el green	*green*
el hoyo	*hole*
el palo	*club*
el hierro	*iron*
la madera	*wood*
el putter	*putter*
la pelota	*ball*
el tee	*tee*

el adversario	*opponent*
la pareja	*partner*
el partido	*match*
el individual femenino	*ladies' singles*
el individual masculino	*men's singles*
el juego de dobles	*doubles*
los dobles mixtos	*mixed doubles*

El ciclismo *Cycling*

la bicicleta de carreras	*racing bike*
la bicicleta de montaña	*mountain bike*
la bomba	*pump*
la cadena	*chain*

la línea	*line*
la pelota	*ball*
la pista	*court*
la raqueta	*racket*
la red	*net*

9 El ocio y los deportes *Hobbies and sports*

una cámara de aire
  de repuesto   *spare inner tube*
el ciclismo de
  montaña   *mountain biking*
los engranajes   *gears*
los frenos   *brakes*
el manillar   *handlebars*
los pedales   *pedals*
el pinchazo   *puncture*
los radios   *spokes*
las ruedas   *wheels*
el sillín   *saddle*

el casco   *helmet*
el maillot   *shirt*
el pantalón
  corto   *cycling shorts*
los guantes   *gloves*
las zapatillas   *shoes*

El atletismo *Athletics*

los bloques de salida
                blocks
los competidores *competitors*
el/la cronometrador-a
                timekeeper
el estadio   *stadium*
la pista   *track*
las pruebas de campo
                field events

el lanzamiento . . .   *throwing . . .*
  de disco   *the discus*
  de martillo   *the hammer*
  de jabalina   *the javelin*
  de peso   *(putting) the shot*

Los deportes náuticos *Water sports*

la natación   *swimming*

braza   *breast stroke*

la carrera de relevos
                relay race
el maratón   *marathon*
la marcha   *walking*
el salto   *jump*
el salto de
  longitud   *long jump*
el salto
  de altura   *high jump*
el salto
  con pértiga   *pole vault*
el triple salto   *triple jump*
la carrera a campo
  traviesa   *cross country*

el/la juez   *judge*
el/la cronometrador-a
                time keeper

las pruebas de pista
                track events
las vallas   *hurdles*
el biatlón   *biathlon*
la carrera   *running race*
el cronómetro   *stop watch*
la vuelta   *lap*
el pistoletazo
  de salida   *starting gun*

estilo libre   *free style*
espalda   *back stroke*
mariposa   *butterfly*
el largo   *length*
el relevo   *relay*
las aletas   *flippers*

9 El ocio y los deportes *Hobbies and sports*

el bañador	swimming costume	la quilla	keel
las gafas	goggles	el timón	rudder
el gorro de		la vela	sail
natación	swimming hat	las vergas	spars
el tubo de			
respiración	snorkel	estribor	starboard
la crema bronceadora		babor	port
resistente	water-resistant		
al agua	sun-cream	zozobrar	capsize

El esquí acuático
Water skiing

el salto de
trampolín *diving*
el salto *dive*
el trampolín *diving board*

la embarcación	
a motor	motor boat
fuera-borda	outboard

el submari-
nismo *underwater diving*
la botella
de oxígeno *oxygen cylinder*
el traje isotérmico
wet suit

Los deportes de invierno
Winter sports

el esquí	skiing
el esquí alpino	alpine skiing
el esquí nórdico/	nordic / cross
de fondo	country skiing
el bastón	
de esquiar	ski stick
las botas	
de esquiar	ski boots
el descenso	downhill race
el eslálom	slalom
los esquíes	skis
la estación	
de esquí	ski resort
el mono	salopette
la pista	piste
la telesilla	ski lift

El piragüismo *Canoeing*

el bote de remos	rowing boat
el chaleco	
salvavidas	life jacket
el kayac	kayak
la pala	paddle
la piragua	canoe
la popa	stern
el remo	rowing
los remos	oars
el timón	helm

La vela *Sailing*

el barco de vela	sailing boat
la caña de timón	tiller
el dingui; la lancha	
neumática	dinghy
la escota	sheet
las maromas	ropes
la orza de	
deriva	centreboard

la pista de	
tobogán	toboggan run
el salto de esquí	ski jumping
el tobogán	toboggan
los patines	skates
el patinaje	
artístico	ice dance

el patinaje sobre hielo	*ice skating*	el hockey sobre hielo	*ice hockey*
la pista de patinaje	*skating rink*	los palos de hockey	*hockey sticks*
		la portería	*goal*
		el puck	*puck*

10 El cuerpo, la salud y las enfermedades
The body, health and sickness

EL CUERPO
THE BODY

Las partes del cuerpo
Parts of the body

el cuerpo	the body
la cara	face
la cabeza	head
la garganta	throat
el cuello	neck
el hombro	shoulder
el brazo	arm
el codo	elbow
la muñeca	wrist
el puño	fist
la mano	hand
el dedo	finger
el pulgar	thumb
el dedo anular	ring finger
el dedo meñique	little finger
el dedo índice	index finger
la uña	fingernail
el tórax	chest
el pecho	bust
la costilla	rib
el costado	side
la espalda	back
la cintura	waist
las caderas	hips
el pene	penis
los testículos	testicles
la pierna	leg
el muslo	thigh
la rodilla	knee
la pantorrilla	calf
el talón	ankle
el pie	foot
el talón	heel
la planta del pie	sole
el dedo del pie	toe
la piel	skin
el hueso	bone
la articulación	joint

la columna vertebral	spine
el esqueleto	skeleton
el cráneo	skull

Los órganos internos
Internal organs

el cerebro	brain
el corazón	heart
el cuello	
del útero	cervix
el estómago	stomach
el hígado	liver
los intestinos	intestines
el ligamento	ligament
el músculo	muscle
el nervio	nerve
la próstata	prostrate
los pulmones	lungs
los riñones	kidneys
la sangre	blood
la arteria	artery
el vaso	
sanguíneo	blood vessel
la vena	vein
el pulso	pulse
el sistema	
nervioso	nervous system
el tendón	tendon
el útero	womb
la vagina	vagina

andar	to walk
arrodillarse	to kneel
correr	to run
descansar	to rest
dormir	to sleep
estar de pie	to stand
hacer ejercicio	to exercise
hacer footing	to jog
respirar	to breathe
saltar	to jump
sentarse	to sit
tumbarse	to lie down

10 El cuerpo, la salud y las enfermedades
The body, health and sickness

LAS MOLESTIAS Y LOS DOLORES ACHES AND PAINS

Me duele.	*It hurts.*
Tengo dolor de ...	*I've got ...*
espalda	*backache*
oídos	*earache*
cabeza	*a headache*
muelas	*toothache*
Tengo ...	*I've got ...*
un dedo inflamado	*a sore finger*
una ampolla	*a blister*

La cara *The face*

		la nariz	*nose*
		la oreja	*ear*
la barbilla	*chin*	el ojo	*eye*
la boca	*mouth*	el cristalino	*lens*
la ceja	*eyebrow*	el iris	*iris*
el cutis	*complexion*	la retina	*retina*
los dientes	*teeth*	el párpado	*eyelid*
la frente	*forehead*	el pelo	*hair*
los labios	*lips*	la pestaña	*eyelash*
la lengua	*tongue*	la piel	*skin*
la mejilla	*cheek*		

Tengo ...	*I've got ...*
un grano/granos	*a spot / spots*
un forúnculo	*a boil*
una espinilla	*a blackhead*
un poro obstruido	*a blocked pore*
un oído obstruido	*a blocked ear*
cerilla en los oídos	*ear wax*
la nariz atascada	*a stuffy nose*
un catarro	*catarrh*
caspa	*dandruff*

estornudar	to sneeze	sonreír	to smile
fruncir el ceño	to frown	toser	to cough
hacer muecas	to grimace; make a face		

EL ASEO Y LA COSMÉTICA
TOILETRIES AND COSMETICS

¿Tiene(-s) un-a/mi(-s) . . . ?	Have you got a / my / some . . . ?
bolsa de aseo	sponge bag
brocha de afeitar	shaving brush
cepillo de dientes	toothbrush
cepillo del pelo	hairbrush
cera para el vello	leg wax
champú	shampoo
compresas	sanitary towels
condón	condom
crema bronceadora	sun cream
crema de afeitar	shaving cream
crema facial	face cream
crema suavizante para el cabello	conditioner
crema/loción hidratante	moisturiser
cuchilla	razor
desodorante	deodorant
elixir bucal	mouth wash
esponja	sponge
jabón	soap
laca de uñas	nail varnish
lima para las uñas	nail file
loción para después del afeitado	after shave
manopla	face cloth
maquinilla eléctrica	electric shaver
pañuelo de papel	paper handkerchief
peine	comb
pinzas	tweezers
polvos de talco	talcum powder
quitaesmalte	nail varnish remover
secador	hair dryer
tampón	tampon
tijeras de las uñas	nail scissors

cepillar	*to brush*	la crema/loción desmaquilladora	
colocar	*to put on*		*make-up remover*
lavar	*to wash*	el lápiz de labios	*lipstick*
limpiar	*to clean*	el lápiz de ojos	*eye liner*
usar	*to use*	el maquillaje	*make-up*
		los polvos	*face powder*
pintarse	*to varnish*	el rímel	*mascara*
las uñas	*one's nails*	la sombra	
quitarse la laca		de ojos	*eye shadow*
de uñas	*to remove varnish*		

La cosmética *Cosmetics*

		lavar/secar	*to wash / dry*
		el pelo	*your hair*
la brocha para		maquillarse	*to put make up on*
maquillaje	*make up brush*	desmaquillarse	*take make up off*
el colorete	*blusher*		

¡OTRA VEZ!

● *Activity:* Unscramble the anagrams.
  ¿Tienes mi(-s) . . . ? *Have you got my . . . ?*

banój   epien   posjean

znispa   dsareco

---

10 El cuerpo, la salud y las enfermedades
The body, health and sickness

LAS ENFERMEDADES
ILLNESSES

¡Que te mejores!	*Get well soon!*

la salud	*health*
en forma	*fit*
saludable	*healthy*
infeccioso-a	*infectious*
la enfermedad	*disease / illness*
la fiebre	*fever*
enfermo-a	*ill*
el mareo	*sickness*
estar mareado-a	*to feel sick*
el dolor	*pain*
la medicina	*medicine*

inflamado-a;	
que duele; doloroso-a	
	sore; painful

Las enfermedades
Illnesses and indisposition

la acidez	*heart burn*
la anorexia	*anorexia*
la apendicitis	*appendicitis*
la apoplejía	*stroke*
la artritis	*arthritis*
el asma	*asthma*
el brazo roto	*broken arm*
la bulimia	*bulimia*
el cáncer	*cancer*
la catarata	*cataract*
la celulitis	*cellulite*
la cicatriz	*scar*
el cólera	*colera*
la conmoción	*shock*
la contusión	*bruising*
la costra	*scab*
la dermatitis	*dermatitis*
la diabetes	*diabetes*
la diarrea	*diarrhoea*
la difteria	*diptheria*

el dolor	
muscular	*muscular pain*
el eczema	*eczema*
las enfermedades	
venéreas	*venereal diseases*
el estreñimiento	*constipation*
el estrés	*stress*
la fiebre	
amarilla	*yellow fever*
la fiebre;	
la calentura	*temperature*
la gripe	*flu*
la halitosis	*halitosis*
la hemofilia	*haemophilia*
la hemorragia	*haemorrage*
las hemorroides	*haemorroides*
la hepatitis	*hepatitis*
la hernia	*hernia*
la indigestión	*indigestion*
la infección	*infection*
la malaria	*malaria*
el mareo	*travel sickness*
la meningitis	*meningitis*
la menopausia	*menopause*
la obesidad	*obesity*
las paperas	*mumps*
el picor	*itching*
el pie de atleta	*athlete's foot*
la pierna rota	*broken leg*
la polio	*polio*
la quemadura	*burn*
la quemadura	
de sol	*sunburn*
la rabia	*rabies*
el reúma	*rheumatism*
la rubéola	*German measles*
el sarampión	*measles*
el sero positivo	*HIV positive*
el SIDA	*AIDS*
la tensión	
arterial	*low / high*
alta/baja	*blood pressure*
el tétano	*tetanus*

la tuberculosis	*tuberculosis*		el miembro	
la varicela	*chicken pox*		artificial	*artificial limb*
			la enfermedad	
la bacteria	*bacteria*		crónica	*chronic illness*
la infección	*infection*		la enfermedad	
el virus	*virus*		intermitente	*spasmodic illness*
ciego-a	*blind*		la enfermera	*nurse*
cojo-a	*lame*		el/la	
minusválido-a	*handicapped*		fisioterapeuta	*physiotherapist*
mudo-a	*dumb*		el/la médico	*doctor*
parapléjico-a	*paraplegic*		el/la óptico	*optician*
sordo-a	*deaf*		el/la osteópata	*osteopath*
			el/la podólogo-a	*chiropodist*
la silla				
de ruedas	*wheel chair*		un ambulatorio	*surgery*
			una cita	*appointment*

10 El cuerpo, la salud y las enfermedades
The body, health and sickness

EN EL MÉDICO *AT THE DOCTORS*

¿Puedo concertar una cita?	*Can I make an appointment?*
Me siento mal/enfermo-a.	*I feel ill.*
Me siento mareado-a.	*I feel sick.*
Tengo . . .	*I have . . .*
dolor de estómago	*stomach ache*
dolor de garganta	*a sore throat*
fiebre	*a temperature*
un resfriado	*a cold*
tos	*a cough*
¿Puede darme algo para . . . ?	*Can I have something for . . . ?*
el dolor de cabeza	*a headache*
enviar al especialista	*to refer to a consultant*
hacerse un análisis	*to have an analysis done*
recetar un tratamiento	*to prescribe treatment*
recetar medicación	*to prescribe medication*
tomar la tensión arterial	*to take ones blood pressure*
tomar una muestra	*to take a sample*
tomarse la temperatura	*to take ones temperature*
tomarse el pulso	*to take ones pulse*

EN EL DENTISTA
AT THE DENTIST

la clínica dental	*dental surgery*
el/la dentista	*dentist*
la enfermera dental	*dental nurse*
la encía	*gum*
el diente; la muela	*tooth*
la raíz	*root*
el colmillo	*canine*

el diente de leche	*milk tooth*
los dientes postizos; la dentadura postiza	*false teeth; dentures*
el empaste	*filling*
el incisivo	*incisor*
la mandíbula superior/inferior	*upper / lower jaw*
el molar	*molar*
la muela del juicio	*wisdom tooth*
el (aparato) corrector	*brace*

126

10 El cuerpo, la salud y las enfermedades
The body, health and sickness

Tengo . . .	I have . . .
dolor de muelas	toothache
un absceso	an abscess
Se me ha caído/roto . . .	I have lost / broken . . .
un diente	a tooth
un empaste	a filling
una funda	a cap
un puente	a bridge

el cepillo de dientes	toothbrush		la pasta dentífrica	toothpaste
la seda dental			el palillo de dientes	tooth pick
	dental floss			

LOS TRATAMIENTOS Y LAS CURAS
TREATMENT AND REMEDIES

Los primeros auxilios
First aid

los apósitos adhesivos; las tiritas	sticking plaster
el botiquín	medicine cabinet
el cabestrillo	sling
la escayola	plaster / cast
la gasa	lint
el imperdible	safety pin
las pinzas	tweezers
las tijeras	scissors
la venda	bandage
el corte	cut
el hematoma	bruise
la herida	wound
la quemadura	burn

Los medicamentos
Medicines

el antibiótico	antibiotic
los comprimidos	tablets
los comprimidos . . .	. . . tablets
antiinflamatorios	anti-inflammatory
contra la malaria	anti-malaria
la crema	cream
la crema antiséptica	antiseptic cream
la crema anti-histamínica	anti-histamine cream
las gotas	drops
las infusiones	infusions
el inhalador	inhaler
las pastillas	lozenges
la píldora	the Pill
las píldoras	pills

10 El cuerpo, la salud y las enfermedades
The body, health and sickness

los somníferos	*sleeping pills*
los supositorios	*suppository*
los tranquilizantes	
	tranquillizers
el vendaje	*dressing*

Otros remedios
Other remedies

la medicina alternativa	*alternative medicine*
la acupuntura	*acupuncture*
la aromaterapia	*aromatherapy*
la fisioterapia	*physiotherapy*
la homeopatía	*homeopathy*
la reflexología	*reflexology*

EL HOSPITAL
HOSPITAL

la ambulancia	*ambulance*
la clínica; el centro médico; el ambulatorio	*clinic*
el/la cirujano	*surgeon*
el/la especialista	*consultant*
el/la ginecólogo	*gynaecologist*
el/la ortodoncista	*orthodontist*
el/la pediatra	*paediatrician*
el/la médico	*doctor*
la enfermera	*nurse*
el/la paciente	*patient*
la cama	*bed*
la camilla	*stretcher*
la sala	*ward*

la dieta	*diet*
la fibra dietética	*dietary fibre*
seguir una dieta equilibrada	*follow a healthy diet*
adelgazar/ engordar	*to lose / gain weight*
ayunar	*to fast*
hacer ejercicio	*to exercise*
atragantarse	*to choke*
desmayarse; perder el sentido	*to faint*
esterilizar	*to sterilise*
infectar	*to infect*
padecer	*to suffer*
el/la anestesista	*anaesthetist*
la anestesia local/general	*local / general anaesthetic*
la cirugía	*surgery*
el escalpelo	*scalpel*
el goteo	*drip*
el instrumental	*instruments*
el láser	*laser*
la medicina intravenosa	*intravenous medicine*
la operación	*operation*
el quirófano	*operating theatre*
la radiografía	*an x-ray*
la convalecencia	*convalescence*
la recuperación	*recuperation*
convalecer	*to convalesce*
doler	*to hurt*
escayolar	*to plaster*
inocular	*to inoculate*
mejorar	*to improve*
operar	*to operate*
sentirse bien	*to feel well*

sentirse		tener náuseas;	
mal/enfermo-a	*to feel ill*	vomitar	*to be sick; vomit*
		vacunar	*to vaccinate*

EL TABACO, LAS DROGAS Y EL ALCOHOL
SMOKING, DRUGS AND ALCOHOL

Prohibido fumar   *No smoking*

El/la fumador-a/no fumador-a
Smoker/non-smoker

el alquitrán	*tar*
el cenicero	*ashtray*
las cerillas	*matches*
los cigarrillos	*cigarettes*
los cigarros puros;	
habanos	*cigars*
el mechero	*lighter*
la nicotina	*nicotine*
el papel	
de fumar	*cigarette paper*
la pipa	*pipe*
el tabaco	*tobacco*
el cáncer	*cancer*
el enfisema	*emphysema*
fumar	*to smoke*
dejar de fumar	*to give up smoking*
fumar menos	*to cut down on smoking*
inhalar; aspirar	
el humo	*to inhale*

Las drogas *Drugs*

el cannabis	*cannabis*
el hachís	*hashish*
la marihuana	*marijuana*
la cocaína	*cocaine*
el crack	*crack*
la heroína	*heroin*
el éxtasis	*ecstasy*
las anfetaminas	*amphetamines*
las drogas	
blandas	*soft drugs*
las drogas duras	*hard drugs*
las drogas de	
diseño	*designer drugs*
inyectarse	*to inject*
la aguja	*needle*
la jeringuilla	*syringe*
la drogadicción	*drug addiction*
el síndrome de	*withdrawal*
la abstinencia	*symptoms*
el mono	*cold turkey*
el/la drogadicto-a	*drug addict*
la toxicomanía	*drug abuse*

10 El cuerpo, la salud y las enfermedades
The body, health and sickness

El alcohol *Alcohol*

El/ella bebe demasiado. — *He / she drinks too much.*

desalcoholizarse — *to dry out*

dejar de beber — *to give up drinking*

el/la abstemio-a — *teetotaller*

el/la alcohólico-a — *alcoholic*

Si bebes no conduzcas	*Don't drink and drive*

11 Las instituciones *Institutions*

LA BANCA Y LA BOLSA
BANKING AND FINANCE

El dinero y el banco
Money and the bank

el banco	*bank*
la caja	
de ahorros	*savings bank*
la sociedad de	
préstamo	
inmobiliario	*building society*
la sucursal	*branch*
el billete	*banknote*
la caja	*till*
el/la cajero-a	*cashier*
el cajero	
automático	*cash machine*
el cambio	*change*
el cambio de	
divisa	*currency rates*
el cheque;	
el talón	*cheque*
la comisión (por	
servicio bancario)	
	commission
el crédito	*credit*
la cuenta	
bancaria	*bank account*
la cuenta	
corriente	*current account*
la cuenta	
de ahorros	*savings account*
el débito	*debit*
el depósito	*deposit*
el dinero	*money*
las divisas	*foreign currency*
en números	
rojos	*in the red*
el estado	
de cuenta	*statement*
la firma	*signature*

la hipoteca	*mortgage*
la identificación	*identification*
la letra bancaria	*banker's draft*
la libra	
esterlina	*pound*
la libreta	
de ahorros	*savings book*
la moneda	*currency*
el número de	
sucursal	
bancaria	*bank sort code*
el préstamo	*loan*
la retirada de fondos	
de un banco	*withdrawal*
el saldo	*balance*
el saldo deudor	*overdraft*
la tarjeta	
de crédito	*credit card*
la tarjeta de identidad	
bancaria	*cheque card*
la transferencia	
bancaria	*transfer*
el billete	
falsificado	*forged note*
el cheque	
abierto	*open cheque*
el cheque	*cheque payable*
al portador	*to the bearer*
el cheque	
cruzado	*crossed cheque*
el cheque	
de viaje	*traveller's cheque*
el cheque	
en blanco	*blank cheque*
el cheque nulo	*invalid cheque*
la falsificación	*forgery*
cambiar dinero	*to change money*
cobrar un cheque	*to cash a cheque*
depositar	*to deposit*
devolver;	
reintegrar	*to pay back; repay*

falsificar	*to forge*
ingresar	*to pay in*
prestar	*to lend*
tomar prestado	*to borrow*

La bolsa *Stock Exchange*

la acción	*share*
el activo	*asset*
el beneficio	*profit*
el capital	*capital*
el certificado	*certificate*
la compra	*purchase*
el coste de vida	*cost of living*
la depreciación	*depreciation*
la deuda	*debt*
los gastos	*expenses*
el índice	*index*
la inflación	*inflation*
el interés	*interest*
el inventario; el capital comercial	*stock*
la inversión	*investment*
el pago	*payment*
el porcentaje	*percentage*
el préstamo	*loan*
el presupuesto	*budget*
el recibo	*receipt*
la suma; la cantidad	*sum*
el valor	*value*
la venta	*sale*
el mercado bajista	*bear market*
el mercado alcista	*bull market*

Los valores *Stocks and shares*

alimentación	*food*
banca	*banking*
comunicaciones	*communications*
construcción	*construction*
electricidad	*electricity*
inversión	*investment*
químicas	*chemicals*
sidero-metalúrgicas	*mining*

la desgravación fiscal	*tax allowances*
el impuesto	*tax*
el impuesto sobre la renta	*income tax*
el interés	*interest*
el IVA	*VAT*

Las divisas *Currencies*

el mercado de divisas	*currency market*
el billete	*note*
la moneda	*coin*
el/la comprador-a	*buyer*
el/la vendedor-a	*seller*
el dólar EE.UU	*American dollar*
el dólar australiano	*Australian dollar*
el franco francés/suizo	*French / Swiss franc*
la libra esterlina	*pound sterling*
la lira	*lire*
el marco alemán	*Deutschmark*
la peseta	*peseta*
el yen	*yen*
ahorrar	*to save*
cobrar intereses	*to charge interest*

11 Las instituciones *Institutions*

comprar	*to buy*	prestar	*to lend*
costar	*to cost*	tomar prestado	*to borrow*
gastar	*to spend*	valer	*to be worth*
invertir	*to invest*	vender	*to sell*
pagar	*to pay*		
pagar impuestos	*to pay tax*	barato-a	*cheap*
perder	*to lose*	costoso-a; caro-a	*dear; expensive*

LA IGLESIA Y LA RELIGIÓN *CHURCH AND RELIGION*

la religión	*religion*	el Hinduismo	*Hinduism*
		el Islamismo	*Islam*
el Budismo	*Buddhism*	el Judaísmo	*Judaism*
el Catolicismo	*Catholicism*		
el Cristianismo	*Christianity*		

Soy . . .	*I am . . .*
ateo-a	*an atheist*
agnóstico-a	*an agnostic*
budista	*a Buddhist*
católico-a	*a Catholic*
cristiano-a	*a Christian*
cuáquero-a	*a Quaker*
hinduista	*a Hindu*
judío-a	*a Jew*
musulmán-ana	*a Moslem*
testigo de Jehová	*a Jehovah's witness*

Alá	*Allah*	el cardenal	*cardinal*
Buda	*Buddha*	el/la discípulo-a	*disciple*
Cristo	*Christ*	el imán	*imam*
Dios	*God*	el mártir	*martyr*
el Espíritu		el mesías	*messiah*
Santo	*Holy Ghost*	la monja	*nun*
Mahoma	*Mohammed*	el monje	*monk*
Moisés	*Moses*	el obispo	*bishop*
la Virgen María	*the Virgin Mary*	el Papa	*the Pope*
		el pastor	*minister*
el apóstol	*apostle*	el/la pecador-a	*sinner*
el arzobispo	*archbishop*	el/la peregrino-a	*pilgrim*

11 Las instituciones *Institutions*

el profeta	*prophet*
el rabino	*rabbi*
el sacerdote	*priest*
el/la santo-a	*saint*
el vicario	*vicar*

la bendición	*blessing*
la comunión	*communion*
el culto; el oficio religioso	*service*
el himno	*hymn*
la misa	*mass*
el motete	*anthem*
la oración; el rezo	*prayer*
el salmo	*psalm*
el sermón	*sermon*

la aguja	*spire*
el altar	*altar*
la capilla	*chapel*
la catedral	*cathedral*
el coro	*choir*
la cúpula	*cupola*
la iglesia	*church*
la mezquita	*mosque*
la nave	*nave*
la sinagoga	*synagogue*
el templo	*temple*

la cruz	*cross*
la vela	*candle*

el ángel	*angel*
el demonio	*devil*

el cielo	*heaven*
la condenación	*damnation*
el infierno	*hell*
el nirvana	*Nirvana*
el paraíso	*paradise*
el purgatorio	*purgatory*
la salvación	*salvation*

la creencia	*belief*
la creación	*creation*
la fe	*faith*
la guerra santa	*Holy war*
el milagro	*miracle*
la peregrinación	*pilgrimage*

absolver	*to absolve*
arrepentirse	*to repent*
cantar	*to sing; chant*
confesarse	*to confess*
convertir/-se	*to convert*
creer/no creer	*to believe / not believe*
ir a la iglesia; asistir al culto	*to attend church*
ir/asistir a misa	*to go to Mass*
ir en peregrinación	*to make a pilgrimage*
meditar	*to meditate*
orar; rezar	*to pray*
predicar	*to preach*
venerar; adorar	*to worship*

11 Las instituciones *Institutions*

LA EDUCACIÓN
EDUCATION

La escuela; el colegio
School

el jardín de infancia	*kindergarten*
la guardería	*play school*
la escuela primaria	*primary school*
la escuela secundaria; el instituto	*secondary school*
el colegio privado	*private school*
el colegio público	*state school*
la universidad laboral	*technical college*
el politécnico	*polytechnic*
la universidad	*university*
el/la alumno-a	*pupil*
el/la estudiante	*student*
el/la director-a	*headmaster / mistress*
el/la subdirector-a	*deputy*
el/la profesor-a	*teacher*
el/la bibliotecario-a	*librarian*
el/la celador-a/ portero-a	*caretaker*
el/la secretario-a	*school secretary*
la clase	*class*
la lección	*lesson*
el recreo	*break*
la matrícula	*registration*

Las asignaturas *Subjects*

el alemán	*German*
el arte	*Art*
la biología	*Biology*
las ciencias	*Science*
la educación física	*P.E.*
el español	*Spanish*
la física	*Physics*
el francés	*French*
la geografía	*Geography*
la historia	*History*
la informática	*I.T.*
el inglés	*English*
las matemáticas	*Mathematics*
la música	*Music*
la química	*Chemistry*
la sociología	*Sociology*
la tecnología	*Technology*
la calificación; la nota; la evaluación	*mark; grade*
la composición	*essay*
la conducta	*behaviour*
los deberes	*homework*
el ejercicio	*exercise*
la escritura	*writing*
el examen	*examination*
el examen escrito	*written examination*
el examen oral	*oral examination*
el informe	*report*
la lectura	*reading*
la ortografía	*spelling*
la puntuación	*punctuation**
el trabajo escrito	*written work*

(* See also *Arts and the Media*, page 103)

11 Las instituciones *Institutions*

aprender	*to learn*
estudiar	*to study*
repasar	*to revise*
presentarse a	
un examen	*to sit an exam*
aprobar	
un examen	*to pass an exam*
suspender	
un examen	*to fail an exam*
volver a presentarse	
a un examen	*to re-sit an exam*
el certificado;	
el diploma	*certificate*
el título	*qualification*
la licenciatura	*degree*
el/la graduado-a;	
el/la bachiller	*graduate*
el/la licenciado-a	*bachelor*
el doctorado	*doctorate*
el máster	*master's degree*
la tesis doctoral	*thesis*
el/la profesor-a	
universitario-a	
	lecturer
el/la catedrático-a	
	professor
el/la doctor-a	*doctor*

Los estudios universitarios
University subjects

la arqueología	*Archeology*
las ciencias	*Sciences*
el derecho	*Law*
la electrónica	*Electronics*

la filosofía	*Philosphy*
la historia	*History*
la informática	*Information Technology*
la ingeniería	*Engineering*
las lenguas	
clásicas	*Classical Languages*
las lenguas	
modernas	*Modern Languages*
las letras; las	
humanidades	*Humanities*
la medicina	*Medicine*
el periodismo	*Journalism*
la psicología	*Psychology*
la psiquiatría	*Psychiatry*
la sociología	*Sociology*
el paraninfo	*lecture theatre*
el seminario	*seminar room*
el/la candidato-a	*candidate*
el/la examinador-a	
	examiner
el aprobado	*pass mark*
el examen	*exam paper*
la pregunta	*question*
la respuesta	*answer*
el resultado	*result*
el año académico;	
el curso	*school year*
el día libre	*day off*
la emergencia	*emergency*
el nuevo año	
académico;	
el nuevo curso	*new school year*
el semestre	*semester*
el trimestre	*term*
las vacaciones	*holidays*

11 Las instituciones *Institutions*

EL ORDEN PÚBLICO
LAW AND ORDER

El crimen y la policía
Crime and the police

la agresión	*assault*
la alarma antirrobo	*burglar alarm*
el arma	*weapon*
el arma de fuego	*gun; firearm*
el/la asesino-a	*murderer*
el ataque	*attack*
la agresión sexual	*sexual attack*
el atentado contra el pudor/la moral	*indecent assault*
el atraco	*hold-up*
el camello; el traficante	*drug dealer*
el carterista	*pickpocket*
el casco	*helmet*
el cazador furtivo	*poacher*
el chantaje	*blackmail*
el coche-patrulla	*police car*
el/la cómplice	*accomplice*
con violencia	*with violence*
el crimen; el delito	*crime*
el criminal	*criminal*
la detención	*arrest*
la emergencia	*emergency*
el/la espía	*spy*
la falsificación	*forgery*
forzar una entrada	*break in*
el fraude	*fraud*
el/la gamberro-a	*hooligan; yob*
el/la guerrillero-a	*guerrilla*
el hurto	*shoplifting*
el incendio provocado	*arson*

el/la ladrón-a	*thief; burglar*
la multa	*fine*
los narcóticos	*narcotics*
el narcotraficante	*drug dealer*
el narcotráfico	*drugs traffic*
la pandilla	*gang*
la pelea	*fight*
el perista	*receiver; fence*
la pistola	*pistola*
el/la provocador-a de incendio	*arsonist*
el/la rehén	*hostage*
el rescate	*rescue*
el revólver	*revolver*
el robo	*robbery*
el secuestro	*kidnapping*
el secuestro aéreo	*hijacking*
el sistema de seguridad	*security system*
los teléfonos de urgencia	*emergency telephone numbers*
el/la terrorista	*terrorist*
el/la traidor	*traitor*
el/la policía	*police officer*
el uniforme	*uniform*
la urgencia	*emergency*
el veneno	*poison*
amenazar	*to threaten*
apuñalar	*to stab*
asesinar	*to murder*
atacar	*to attack*
atracar	*to hold up*
buscar	*to search*
disparar	*to shoot*
engañar	*to deceive*
espiar	*to spy*
hacer trampas	*to cheat*
matar	*to kill*
pegar	*to mug*
procesar	*to prosecute*
robar	*to burgle; rob*
violar	*to rape*

11 Las instituciones *Institutions*

Ante los tribunales *In court*

el/la abogado	*lawyer*
la absolución	*acquittal*
el acta	*act*
la apelación	*appeal*
el banquillo (de los acusados)	*dock*
los cargos	*charges*
el caso	*case*
la celda	*cell*
la condena a perpetuidad	*life sentence*
la culpabilidad	*guilt*
culpable	*guilty*
los daños	*damages*
el delito menor	*minor offence*
la demanda	*complaint*
el/la detenido-a; el/la acusado-a	*prisoner*
el fallo provisional	*decree nisi*
la fianza	*bail*
inocente	*innocent*
el interrogatorio	*interrogation*
el/la juez	*judge*

el juicio	*prosecution*
el jurado	*jury*
el juramento	*oath*
la ley	*law*
la libertad bajo fianza	*release on bail*
la libertad condicional	*probation*
la multa	*fine*
la ofensa	*offence*
la orden judicial	*warrant*
la prisión	*prison*
el secretario	*clerk of the court*
la sentencia	*sentence*
el tribunal de justicia	*law court*
el veredicto	*verdict*
confesar	*confess*
declararse culpable	*to plead guilty*
declararse inocente	*to plead innocent*
jurar	*to swear*
ser testigo	*to witness*

11 Las instituciones *Institutions*

EL EJÉRCITO
THE MILITARY

Las Fuerzas Armadas
The Armed Forces

la guerra	*war*
declarar	
la guerra	*to declare war*
la paz	*peace*
firmar un	*to sign a peace*
tratado de paz	*treaty*
el acuerdo	*agreement*
el aliado	*ally*
el alto el fuego	*ceasefire*
la amenaza	*threat*
el asalto	*assault*
el ataque	*attack*
la batalla	*battle*
el bloqueo	*blockade*
el enemigo	*enemy*
las fuerzas de	
pacificación	*peacekeeping*
	troops
el golpe	*coup*
la Guerra Fría	*Cold War*
la rendición	*surrender*
el repliegue	*withdrawal*
la retirada	*retreat*
las sanciones	*sanctions*
el/la terrorista	*terrorist*
las tropas de las	*United Nations*
Naciones Unidas	*forces*
el casco	*helmet*
el vehículo	*vehicle*
la vigilancia	*surveillance*

El ejército de tierra *The army*

la artillería	*artillery*
el campamento	*camp*

el capitán general	
del ejército	*field marshall*
la comandancia	*command*
la compañía	*company*
el coronel	*colonel*
el cuartel	*barracks*
el cuartel	
general	*HQ*
el general	*general*
la infantería	*infantry*
la ley marcial	*court martial*
el lugarteniente	*lieutenant*
el objetor de	*conscientious*
conciencia	*objector*
el oficial	*officer*
el sargento	*sergeant*
el servicio militar;	
la mili	*military service*
el centinela	*sentry*
la graduación	*rank*
la patrulla	*patrol*
el recluta	*recruit*
el soldado	*soldier; private*
el tanque	*tank*
el transporte	
de tropas	*personnel carrier*
las tropas	*troops*

La marina *The navy*

el almirante	*admiral*
el astillero	
naval	*naval dockyard*
el buque de	
guerra	*battleship*
el capitán	*captain*
el crucero	*cruiser*
la flota	*fleet*
la fragata	*frigate*
el marinero	*sailor*
el piloto	*pilot*
el portaaviones	*aircraft carrier*

el submarino	*submarine*	las armas	
la tripulación	*crew*	químicas	*chemical weapons*
el vigía	*watch*	las armas	
		nucleares	*nuclear weapons*

La aviación *The air force*

el aviador	*airman*
el avión	
a reacción	*jet*
la base aérea	*air force base*
el caza	*fighter (plane)*
el copiloto	*co-pilot*
el escuadrón	*squadron*
el helicóptero	*helicopter*
el manteni-	
miento	*maintenance*
el navegante	*navigator*
el piloto	*pilot*
el radar	*radar*

Las armas *Weapons*

la ametralla-	
dora	*machine gun*
el arma de	
fuego	*gun*

la bomba	*bomb*
la granada	
de mano	*hand grenade*
la mina	*mine*
el misil	*missile*
el misil de crucero	
	cruise missile
el misil	
teledirigido	*guided missile*
el mortero	*mortar*
el objetivo	*target*
el proyectil	*shell*
el revólver	*revolver*
el rifle	*rifle*
el torpedo	*torpedo*

bombardear	*to bomb*
defender	*to defend*
disparar	*to shoot*
luchar	*to fight*
navegar	*to sail*
volar	*to fly*

11 **Las instituciones** *Institutions*

LA POLÍTICA Y EL GOBIERNO
POLITICS AND GOVERNMENT

El gobierno municipal
Local government

la alcaldía	*town council*
el alcalde	*mayor*
la alcaldesa	*mayoress*
asuntos sociales	*social services*
el ayuntamiento	*town hall*
los concejales	*town councillors*
la contribución municipal	*rates*
la corporación municipal	*elected representatives*
el jefe del ejecutivo	*chief executive*

la junta municipal	*council meeting*
los impuestos municipales	*local taxes*
la oficina de empleo	*employment office*

El gobierno nacional
National government

el Congreso de los Diputados	*House of Commons*
los Cortes	*Parliament*
el/la diputado-a	*member of parliament*
el Senado	*Senate*
el distrito electoral	*constituency*
la economía	*economy*
la elección	*election*
el escaño	*seat of parliament*
el gobierno	*government*

el Ministerio de . . .	*Ministry of . . .*
el/la ministro-a de . . .	*Minister of . . .*
Agricultura, Pesca y Alimentación	*Agriculture, Fisheries and Food*
Asuntos Sociales	*Social Affairs*
Cultura	*Heritage*
Defensa	*Defence*
Educación y Ciencia	*Education and Science*
Empleo y Seguridad Social	*Employment*
Hacienda y Economía	*Finance*
Interior	*Home Office*
Obras Públicas, Transportes y Medio Ambiente	*Transport and Environment*
Salud y Consumo	*Health and Safety*

el partido	*party*
el/la político-a	*politician*
el/la presidente	*president*
el/la presidente del gobierno	*prime minister*
el cónsul	*consul*

el diplomático	*diplomat*
la embajada	*embassy*
el/la embajador-a	*ambassador*
el/la enviado-a	*envoy*

someter a
   debate   *to debate*
sondear   *to canvass*

tomar la
   palabra   *to speak*
votar   *to vote*

la ciudad	town / city	la ciudad industrial	industrial town
la ciudad de interés histórico	historical town	el puerto	port

EL CENTRO
THE TOWN CENTRE

el aparcamiento	car park	la plaza del mercado	market place
el ayuntamiento	town hall	el polideportivo	leisure centre
el banco	bank	el restaurante	restaurant
el bar	bar	la sala de conciertos	concert hall
la biblioteca	library	la sociedad inmobiliaria	estate agent
el café	cafe	el teatro	theatre
el cine	cinema	el zoo	zoo
la comisaría	police station		
Correos	post office	la acera	pavement
la estación	station	la avenida	avenue
la estación de autobuses/trenes	bus / train station	la calle	street
		la calzada	middle of the road
el estadio de fútbol	football stadium	la carretera	road
el hotel	hotel	el carril para ciclistas	bicycle track
el jardín botánico	botanical gardens	el cruce	intersection
el mercado	market	la glorieta	roundabout
el museo	museum	la indicación; la señal	sign post
el museo de pinturas	art gallery	la parada de autobuses	bus stop
la oficina de turismo	tourist office	el paso de cebra	pedestrian crossing
la oficina del ayuntamiento	council office	el paso elevado	level crossing
el parque	park	el paso subterráneo	subway
la piscina	swimming pool	el semáforo	traffic lights
la plaza de toros	bull ring	la zona peatonal	pedestrian area

12 La ciudad y las compras *Town and shopping*

LAS TIENDAS Y LAS COMPRAS
SHOPS AND SHOPPING

la agencia de viajes	*travel agent*
la carnicería	*butchers*
la confitería	*sweet shop*
el estanco	*tobacconist*
la farmacia	*chemist*
la ferretería; la droguería	*ironmongers*
la floristería	*flower shop*
la tienda de fotografía	*photographers*
la gasolinera	*petrol station*
los grandes almacenes	*department store*
la panadería	*bakery*
la papelería	*stationers*
la pastelería	*cake shop*
la peluquería	*hairdressers*
la pescadería	*fish shop*
el quiosco	*newsagents*
la tienda de comestibles	*grocers*
la tienda de modas	*clothes shop*
la tintorería	*dry cleaners*
la verdulería; la frutería	*greengrocers*
la zapatería	*shoe shop*
junto a	*next door to*
enfrente (del cine)	*opposite (the cinema)*
en la primera/ siguiente calle ...	*in the first / next street ...*
a la izquierda/ derecha	*on the left / right*
después del semáforo	*after the lights*
cruzando la calle	*across the road*
en la plaza del mercado	*in the marketplace*
en la plaza	*in the square*
en la carretera/ calle	*in the road / street*
allí	*over there*
al volver la esquina	*around the corner*
al otro lado de la calle	*on the other side of the road*

De compras *Shopping*

¿Tiene ... ?	*Have you got ... ?*
Quisiera ...	*I would like ...*
una botella de ...	*a bottle of ...*
un frasco de ...	*a jar of ...*
una caja de ...	*a box of ...*
un paquete de ...	*a packet of ...*
un tubo de ...	*a tube of ...*
un estuche de ...	*a case of ...*
un bidón de ...	*a drum of ...*
una lata de ...	*a can / tin of ...*
un sobre de ...	*a sachet of ...*

al natural	*fresh*
enlatado-a	*tinned*
crudo-a	*raw*
cocido-a	*cooked*
¿Cuánto?	*How much?*
un kilo	*a kilo*
medio kilo	*half a kilo*
un litro	*a litre*
medio litro	*half a litre*
¿Cuánto cuesta?	*How much does it cost?*
Eso es todo.	*That's all.*
Gracias.	*Thank you.*
Lo siento, no tengo cambio.	*I'm sorry I haven't any change.*

En los grandes almacenes
In the department store

Planta sótano	***Basement***
Supermercado	*Food Hall*
Menaje-Hogar	*Kitchenware*
Bricolaje	*DIY*
Planta baja	***Ground floor***
Artículos de Piel	*Leather goods*
Papelería	*Stationery*
Música y Radio/ Sonido	*Music and Radio*
Agencia de Viajes	*Travel agents*
Cafetería	*Snack bar*
Perfumería	*Perfumery*
Cosmética	*Cosmetics*
Ropa de Caballero	*Gentlemen's clothing*
Fotografía	*Photography*

Primera planta	***First floor***
Moda	*Fashion*
Lencería; Ropa Interior	*Underwear*
Vestidos	*Dresses*
Trajes	*Suits*
Coordinados	*Separates*
Ropa Deportiva	*Casual wear*
Trajes de Noche	*Evening wear*
Segunda planta	***Second floor***
Ropa de Cama	*Bed linen*
Ropa de Casa	*Household linens*
Porcelana y Cristal	*China and glassware*
Cuberterías	*Cutlery*
Deportes	*Sports and sportswear*
Moda Infantil y Juguetería	*Childrenswear and Toys*
Tercera planta	***Third floor***
Muebles	*Furniture*
Alfombras; Moquetas	*Carpeting*
Cortinas; Coordinados	*Home furnishings*
Electro- domésticos	*Electrical goods*
Ordenadores; Electrónica	*Computers*
Televisión y Vídeos; Imagen	*Television and videos*
Cuarta planta	***Fourth floor***
Restaurante	*Restaurant*
Servicio de atención al cliente	*Customer services*
Servicios; Lavabos	*Toilets*
Oficinas	*Offices*

12 La ciudad y las compras *Town and shopping*

¿Dónde está . . . ?	*Where is the . . . ?*
el ascensor	*lift*
el departamento de . . .	*. . . department*
la escalera mecánica	*escalator*
el mostrador	*counter*
la salida	*exit*
¿Dónde están los probadores?	*Where are the changing rooms?*

Comprando
Making purchases

¿Cuánto es?	*How much is it?*	demasiado grande/	
Es demasiado.	*It's too much.*	pequeño-a	*too big / small*
demasiado		Está	
caro-a	*too expensive*	estropeado-a.	*It's damaged.*

¿Tiene algo . . .	*Have you got anything . . .*
más barato-a?	*cheaper?*
más caro-a?	*more expensive?*
más grande?	*bigger?*
mejor?	*better?*
en (rojo)?	*in (red)?*
¿De dónde es/son?	*Where is it / are they from?*
¿De qué es/son?	*What is it / are they made of?*
¿Puedo probármelo?	*Can I try it on?*
¿Tiene . . .	*Have you got . . .*
una talla más grande/pequeña?	*a size bigger / smaller?*
algo más ancho/estrecho	*something wider / narrower?*
algo más largo/corto?	*something longer / shorter*
(No) me gusta.	*I like / don't like it.*
(No) me está bien.	*It fits / doesn't fit.*
(No) me sienta bien.	*It suits me / doesn't suit me.*
El color/estilo (no) me sienta bien.	*The colour / style suits (doesn't suit) me.*

Me lo/la llevo.	*I'll take it.*
¿Puedo encargar un-a . . . ?	*Can I order a . . . ?*
¿Dónde hay que pagar?	*Where do I pay?*
¿Aceptan tarjetas de crédito?	*Do you take credit cards?*
¿Aceptan un cheque?	*Do you take a cheque?*
No tengo cambio.	*I haven't any change.*
¿A qué hora se abre/cierra?	*What time do you open / close?*
¿Pueden mandarlo a mi hotel?	*Can you send it to my hotel?*
¿Cuándo estará listo?	*When will it be ready?*
¿Pueden arreglar (mi reloj)?	*Can you repair (my watch)*

EN LA PELUQUERÍA
AT THE HAIRDRESSERS

la cola de caballo	*pony tail*
el flequillo	*fringe*
el moldeador	*wave*
el pelo/el cabello	*hair*
la peluca	*wig*
la permanente	*perm*
el postizo	*hair piece*
la trenza	*plait*
corto/largo	*short / long*
ondulado/rizado	*wavy / curly*
lacio; liso	*straight*
con brillo	*shiny*

el acondicionador	*conditioner*
el champú	*shampoo*
la navaja	*razor*
las tijeras	*scissors*
cortar	*to cut*
cortar las puntas	*to trim*
decolorar	*to bleach*
lavar	*to wash*
marcar	*to set*
rizar	*to curl*
secar con secador de mano	*to blow dry*
teñir	*to dye*

12 La ciudad y las compras *Town and shopping*

EN EL BANCO Y EN CORREOS
AT THE BANK AND POST OFFICE

El banco *Bank*

la caja	*cash desk*
el cajero	*cashier*
el cambio	*money exchange*
el departamento de extranjero	*foreign transactions*
la cola	*queue*
la hoja	*form*
el horario	*opening hours*
la ventanilla	*counter*
los billetes	*notes*
el cheque	*cheque*
la divisa	*currency*
el giro postal internacional	*international money order*
en metálico	*in cash*
las monedas	*coins*
el talonario de cheques	*cheque book*
la tarjeta de crédito	*credit card*

Cambiar dinero *Changing money*

Quisiera cobrar un cheque de viaje.	*I would like to cash a traveller's cheque.*
Quisiera cambiar dinero.	*I would like to change some money.*
¿Qué tengo que hacer?	*What do I have to do?*
¿Dónde tengo que ir?	*Where do I have to go?*
¿Dónde hay que firmar?	*Where do I sign?*
¿Dónde puedo cobrar el dinero?	*Where do I get my cash?*
Aquí tiene mi pasaporte/carnet de identidad.	*Here is my passport / identity card.*
¿Cómo funciona el cajero automático?	*How do I operate the cash machine?*
Mi número de identificación personal es . . .	*My PIN number is . . .*
¿Cuánto me dan por . . . ?	*How much do I get for . . . ?*
¿Cuál es el tipo de cambio?	*What is the exchange rate?*
¿Cuánto tengo en mi cuenta?	*How much have I got in my account?*
Quiero sacar dinero.	*I want to withdraw some money.*
Mi nombre/clave es . . .	*My name / code word is . . .*
¿Cuál es mi saldo actual?	*What is my current balance?*
He perdido mi . . .	*I have lost my . . .*
tarjeta de crédito	*credit card*
talonario de cheques	*cheque book*
dinero	*money*

¿Qué puedo hacer?	*What should I do?*
¿Cómo puede ponerme en contacto con . . . ?	*How do I contact . . . ?*

cambiar dinero	*to change money*
cobrar un cheque	*to cash a cheque*
firmar	*to sign*
sacar/retirar dinero	*to withdraw money*

Correos *Post office*

la carta	*letter*
el giro postal	*postal order*
el mostrador	*counter*
el paquete	*parcel*
el sello	*stamp*
el sobre	*envelope*
la tarjeta postal	*postcard*
el telegrama	*telegram*
la ventanilla	*position*

El teléfono *Telephone*

(See *The Company*, page 97 for further telephone vocabulary.)

el aparato; el auricular	*handset*
la cabina de teléfono	*telephone box*
la guía de teléfonos	*directory*
información	*directory enquiries*
la llamada a cobro revertido	*reverse charge call*
el número de teléfono	*telephone number*
el prefijo	*telephone code*
la tarjeta telefónica	*telephone card*
marcar	*dial; tap in*

Quisiera . . .	*I would like . . .*
enviar un telegrama	*to send a telegram*
enviar un fax	*to send a fax*
hacer una llamada de teléfono	*to make a telephone call*
hacer una llamada a cobro revertido	*to make a reverse charge call*
monedas para el teléfono	*change for the telephone*
sellos para una carta/tarjeta para . . .	*stamps for a letter/post card to . . .*

12 La ciudad y las compras *Town and shopping*

LAS DIRECCIONES
DIRECTIONS

¿Donde está . . .?

a la derecha	*on the right*	todo recto/	
a la izquierda	*on the left*	seguido	*straight ahead*

¿Cómo puedo llegar a . . . ?	*How do I get to . . . ?*
¿A qué distancia está?	*How far is it?*
¿Está lejos de aquí?	*Is it far from here?*
¿Está cerca de aquí?	*Is it near here?*

¿Se puede ir andando?	*Can I get there on foot?*
Coja la primera (calle) a la derecha/izquierda.	*You take the first road on the right / left.*
Vaya hasta el cruce/el semáforo/el puente.	*Go to the crossing / lights / bridge.*
Cruce la carretera/el puente/ la plaza.	*Cross the road / bridge / square.*
Coja el paso subterráneo.	*Take the underpass.*
Cuando llegue a . . . gire . . .	*When you come to the . . . you turn . . .*
(No) está lejos.	*It's (not) far.*
Está a cien metros/cinco minutos.	*It's 100 metres / 5 minutes away.*
¿Se puede ir en autobús/coche?	*Can I get there by bus / car?*
Coja . . .	*Take . . .*
el autobús número . . .	*the number . . . bus*
el metro	*the underground*
el tren	*the train*
. . . y bájese en la parada . . .	*. . . and get off at the stop . . .*
¿Cada cuánto tiempo hay trenes?	*How often do the trains run?*
Cada (diez minutos)	*Every (ten minutes)*

150

¿Cuánto cuesta?	*How much does it cost?*
Puede comprar (un bonobús)	*You can buy a (multi journey bus card.)*
¿Dónde puedo comprar uno?	*Where can I get one?*
En correos/un estanco/un quiosco	*At the post office / tobacconist's / kiosk*
¿Dónde está . . . ?	*Where is . . . ?*
Tiene que cancelar/formalizar su billete.	*You have to cancel / validate your ticket.*

Cuando llegue allí, está . . .
   a la izquierda/a la derecha
   dentro del edificio
   al lado de la fuente
   al pie de las escaleras
   frente al parque
   camino del castillo
   frente a la iglesia

When you get there it's . . .
   on the left / right
   inside the building
   beside the fountain
   at the bottom of the steps
   opposite the park
   on the way to the castle
   facing the church

Tiene que ir . . .
   a la izquierda/a la derecha del museo
   a lo largo de la orilla del río
   por el puente
   pasando el monumento

You have to go . . .
   to the left / right of the museum
   along the river bank
   over the bridge
   past the memorial

¡Aquí está!
Está . . .
   por allí
   allí arriba
   allí abajo
   en algún sitio

It's right here!
It's . . .
   over there
   up there
   down there
   somewhere

¡No sé donde está!   *I don't know where it is!*

andar	*to walk*	girar	*to turn*
coger	*to take*	pasar	*to pass*
conducir	*to drive*	seguir	*to follow*
cruzar	*to cross*		

13 Los viajes y el turismo *Travel and tourism*

LOS VIAJES
TRAVEL

la excursión	*excursion*
el horario	*timetable*
la llegada	*arrival*
la salida	*departure*
el tour; el recorrido	
turístico	*tour*
la travesía	*voyage*
el viaje	*journey*

Viajando en tren
Travel by train

el andén	*platform*
el billete	*ticket*
el billete de ida	*single ticket*
el billete de ida	
y vuelta	*return ticket*
el billete con	
descuento	*cheap ticket*
la estación (de	
ferrocarril)	
- RENFE	*station*
la media tarifa	*half fare*
el/la pasajero-a	*passenger*
el retraso	*delay*
la tarifa	
completa	*full fare*
la venta	
automática	*automatic*
de billetes	*ticket sales*

Los trenes   Trains

la AVE (Alta	
Velocidad	*high-speed*
Española)	*intercity train*
el expreso/	
el TALGO	*express*
el mercancías	*freight train*
el motorail	*motorail*
el rápido	*fast train*
el tren correo	*slow / mail train*
el tren de	
cercanías	*local train*
el tren de largo	
recorrido	*Inter-city*
eléctrico	*electric*
diesel	*diesel*
de vapor	*steam*
las agujas	*points*
la cafetería	*buffet car*
el coche-cama	*sleeper*
las líneas eléctricas	
aéreas	*overhead cables*
la litera	*couchette*
el motor	*engine*
los raíles	*rails*
las señales	*signals*
el vagón;	
el coche	*railway carriage*
el vagón-	
restaurante	*restaurant car*
las vías	*lines*

¿Es necesario reservar billete con antelación?	*Do you have to book in advance?*
¿A qué hora sale el tren?	*What time does the train leave?*
¿De qué andén?	*From which platform?*
¿Tengo que hacer transbordo?	*Do I have to change?*
¿Es éste el tren de . . . ?	*Is this the train for . . . ?*

13 Los viajes y el turismo *Travel and tourism*

Fumador	*Smoking*
No Fumador	*Non-smoking*
anular un billete	*to cancel a ticket*
cambiar un billete	*to change a ticket*
formalizar un billete	*to validate a ticket*
reservar con antelación	*to book in advance*
reservar un asiento	*to reserve a seat*
viajar sin billete	*to travel without a ticket*

Viajando en avión
Travel by plane

la aduana	*customs*
el aeropuerto	*airport*
la cinta de equipajes	*luggage carousel*
la clase preferente	*first class*
la clase turista	*economy class*
la etiqueta de equipaje	*luggage label*
la facturación	*check-in*
el formulario de inmigración	*immigration form*
la inmigración	*immigration*
las llegadas	*arrivals*
la puerta número . . .	*gate . . .*
la sala de salidas	*departure lounge*
las salidas	*departures*
la tarjeta de embarque	*boarding card*
la tienda libre de impuestos	*duty-free shop*
el viajero	*passenger*

el viajero en tránsito	*transit passenger*
el vuelo	*flight*
el vuelo chárter	*charter flight*
el vuelo regular	*scheduled flight*
diríjanse al mostrador/ puerta . . .	*go to desk / gate . . .*
el accidente de aviación	*plane crash*
el ala	*wing*
el ascensor	*lift*
el asiento	*seat*
el asiento de pasillo	*aisle / corridor seat*
el asiento de ventanilla	*window seat*
el aterrizaje	*landing*
el aterrizaje forzoso	*crash landing*
los auriculares	*head set*
la avería de motor	*engine trouble*
la azafata	*stewardess*
el bache	*air pocket*
la cabina	*cabin*
el chaleco salvavidas	*life jacket*
el cinturón de seguridad	*safety belt*
la cola	*queue*
la cola (de avión)	*tail*
el control de pasaportes	*passport control*
el copiloto	*second pilot*
el despegue	*take off*
el equipaje	*luggage*
la escalera	*stairs*
los escalones	*steps*
la fila	*row*
el fuselaje	*fuselage*
la hélice	*propeller*

13 Los viajes y el turismo *Travel and tourism*

el jet; el avión a reacción	jet
la mesa	table
el navegante	navigator
las normas de seguridad	safety regulations
el número de asiento	seat number
el pasaporte	passport
el piloto	pilot
la pista	runway
la puerta	door
la salida	way out
la salida de emergencia	emergency exit
la tripulación	crew
la turbulencia	turbulence
aterrizar	to land
despegar	to take off

Viajando en barco
Travel by boat

el contador (de navío)	purser
el crucero	cruise
la cubierta	deck
el ferry	ferry
el oficial de navío	ship's officer

la plancha	gang plank
las puertas de embarque de vehículos	vehicle loading doors
la rampa	ramp
la tripulación	crew
El mar está ...	The sea is ...
revuelto	rough
tranquilo	smooth
navegar	to sail
marearse	to be sea sick
atracar al muelle	to dock

Viajando en autobús
Travel by bus

el asiento	seat
el conductor	driver
la estación de autobuses	bus station
la parada de autobús	bus stop
el pasillo	aisle
el precio del viaje; el billete	fare
el horario de autobuses	bus timetable

¿A qué hora sale/llega el autobús?	What time does the bus leave / arrive?
¿Cuánto vale el billete?	How much is the ticket?
¿De dónde sale el autobús?	Where does the bus leave from?
¿Dónde está la parada?	Where's the bus stop?

13 Los viajes y el turismo *Travel and tourism*

(See also *Hobbies and sports*, page 116.)

VIAJANDO EN BICICLETA/EN MOTO
TRAVEL BY BICYCLE/MOTORBIKE

la bicicleta	*bicycle*
la moto(cicleta)	*motor bike / scooter*
la bomba de bicicleta	*pump*
la cadena	*chain*
la caja de herramientas	*repair kit*
los frenos	*brakes*
el manillar	*handle bars*
el neumático	*tyre*
el pinchazo	*puncture*
las ruedas	*wheels*
el sillín	*saddle*

¡OTRA VEZ!

● *Activity: how do you prefer to travel?*

(a) (b) (c) (d) (e) (f) (g) (h)

13 Los viajes y el turismo *Travel and tourism*

EL TURISMO
TOURISM

la agencia de viajes	*travel agent*
el agroturismo	*country holidays*
la anulación	*cancellation*
los billetes	*tickets*
el folleto	*brochure*
la hoja de reserva	*booking form*
las inyecciones; las vacunas	*jabs; inoculations*
el seguro	*insurance*
el visado	*visa*

Las zonas de veraneo
Holiday areas

el lugar de veraneo; el centro turístico	*holiday resort*
el parque nacional	*national park*
el parque temático	*theme park*

Zonas Populares en España
Popular Areas in Spain

Las Costas	**Coasts**
La Costa del Sol	*(south east Mediterranean)*
La Costa Brava	*(north east Mediterranean)*
La Costa Verde	*(north coast of Spain)*

Las Islas	**Islands**
Las Islas Baleares	*The Balearics*
Las Islas Canarias	*The Canaries*

Las Montañas	**Mountains**
Los Picos de Europa	*(northern Spain, near Santander)*
Los Pirineos	*(between France and Spain)*
La Sierra Nevada	*(southern Spain, near Granada)*
El Coto Donaña	*Doñana National Park (south west Spain)*

Me gusta pasar mis vacaciones . . .	*I like to spend my holidays . . .*
en el campo	*in the country*
en casa	*at home*
en una ciudad	*in a city*
en el mar	*at sea*
en la montaña	*in the mountains*
en la playa	*at the sea-side*
Prefiero . . .	*I prefer . . .*
unas vacaciones tranquilas	*a quiet holiday*
unas vacaciones en el extranjero	*an overseas holiday*
unas vacaciones en la playa	*a seaside holiday*

13 Los viajes y el turismo *Travel and tourism*

unas vacaciones con actividades	*an activity holiday*
un viaje	*a trip*
un tour	*a tour*
un crucero	*a cruise*
viajar de mochila	*back packing*
el senderismo	*a walking holiday*
el descanso de fin de semana	*a weekend holiday*
una excursión	*a day trip*
unas vacaciones llenas de aventuras	*an adventure holiday*
unas vacaciones con mis amigos	*a holiday with my friends*
Quiero ir a sitios de interés turístico.	*I want to see the sights.*

un anfiteatro	*amphitheatre*
un bosque	*forest*
una casa solariega	*stately home*
un castillo	*castle*
una catedral	*cathedral*
unas cuevas	*caves*
un edificio histórico	*historic building*
una iglesia	*church*
un lago	*lake*
el lugar de nacimiento de...	*the birthplace of...*
un mar; un océano	*sea*
una mezquita	*mosque*
un monasterio	*abbey*
una montaña	*mountain*
un monumento	*monument*
un monumento antiguo	*ancient monument*
un museo	*museum*
un puente	*bridge*
un río	*river*
unas ruinas romanas/árabes	*Roman/Moorish ruins*

un valle	*valley*
una vista	*view*
El/la turista	*The tourist*
el/la visitante	*visitor*
el/la viajero-a	*traveller*
el/la que viaja con mochila	*backpacker*
el/la veraneante	*holiday maker*
el/la gamberro-a de litrona	*'lager lout'*
el adaptador eléctrico	*electric adaptor*
las botas/los zapatos para caminar	*walking boots/shoes*
la cámara; máquina de fotos	*camera*
el cinturón para el dinero	*money belt*
la crema para después del sol	*after-sun cream*
la guía	*guide; guide book*
el libro de frases	*phrase book*
la maleta	*suitcase*
el mapa	*map*
la mochila	*ruck sack*
el pasaporte	*passport*

13 Los viajes y el turismo *Travel and tourism*

el plano de la ciudad	*town plan*
el protector solar	*sun cream / lotion*
el repelente de insectos	*insect repellent*
el recuerdo	*souvenir*
la riñonera	*bum bag*

alojarse	*to stay*
comprar	*to buy*
filmar	*to film*
hacer fotos	*to photograph*
ir al extranjero	*to go abroad*
reservar	*to book*
viajar	*to travel*
visitar	*to visit*

El alojamiento *Holiday accommodation*

Vamos a alojarnos en ...	We are going to stay ...
un albergue para jóvenes	*in a youth hostel*
un apartamento	*in an apartment*
un camping	*on a camp site*
una fonda	*at an inn*
una granja	*on a farm*
un hostal	*in a boarding house*
un hotel	*in an hotel*
un parador	*in a parador (luxury state hotel)*
una pensión	*at a guest house*

la pensión completa	*full board*
la media pensión	*half board*
en el hotel	*in the hotel*
el ascensor	*lift*
el bar	*bar*
la cama	*bed*
las escaleras	*stairs*
el gimnasio	*fitness room*
la habitación	*bedroom*

la llave	*key*
la piscina	*pool*
el portero	*porter*
la recepción	*reception*
la reserva	*reservation*
el restaurante	*restaurant*
el comedor	*dining room*
el salón	*lounge*
la tienda	*shop*
el vestuario	*changing room*

una habitación . . .	*a . . . room*
doble	*double*
individual	*single*

una habitación con . . .	*a room with . . .*
aire acondicionado	*air conditioning*
baño	*bath*
ducha	*shower*
instalaciones para minusválidos	*disabled facilities*
teléfono	*phone*
televisión	*TV*
terraza	*balcony*
vistas al mar	*sea view*

¿Qué precio tiene la habitación?	*How much is the room?*
¿Está incluido el desayuno?	*Is breakfast included?*

¿A qué hora se sirve . . .	*What time is . . .*
el desayuno?	*breakfast?*
la comida?	*lunch?*
la cena?	*dinner?*

Quisiera reservar/cancelar una habitación.	*I'd like to reserve / cancel a room.*
Tengo una habitación reservada a nombre de . . .	*I have a room reserved in the name of . . .*

El aire acondicionado no funciona.	*The air conditioning isn't working.*
Necesito otra toalla.	*I need another towel.*
No hay jabón.	*There's no soap.*

En el camping
On the camp-site

el agua	*water*	las duchas	*showers*
el aparcamiento	*parking*	la electricidad	*electricity*
la autocaravana	*camper van*	el emplazamiento	*site*
la basura	*refuse*	los fregaderos	*sinks*
la caravana	*caravan*	el lavadero	*washing facilities*
		los servicios	*toilets*
		la tienda	*tent*

13 Los viajes y el turismo *Travel and tourism*

En el albergue para jóvenes
In the youth hostel

la cocina	*kitchen*
el comedor	*dining room*
el dormitorio	*dormitory*
las normas	*regulations*

el salón	
de recreo	*recreation room*
los servicios	*toilets*
el/la vigilante	*warden*

Rellene la ficha, por favor.   *Fill in the form, please*

Nombre	*Name*
Dirección	*Address*
Lugar de Nacimiento	*Place of birth*
Fecha de Nacimiento	*Date of birth*
Nacionalidad	*Nationality*
Matrícula de Coche	*Car registration*
Fecha de Llegada	*Date of arrival*
Fecha de Salida	*Date of departure*
Número de Carnet de Identidad/ Pasaporte	*Identity card / passport number*

En el mar *At sea*

el acantilado	*cliffs*
la boya	*buoy*
el faro	*lighthouse*
la isla	*island*
el mar	*sea*
el muelle	*dock*
el puerto	*port*
las rocas	*rocks*
la barca	*boat*
el barco	*ship*
el barco de pesca	*fishing boat*

el barco de vapor	*steamship*
el barco rastreador	*trawler*
el buque contenedor	*container ship*
el ferry	*ferry*
la lancha motora	*motor boat*
el submarino	*submarine*
el transatlántico	*cruise liner*
el velero	*sailing ship*
el ancla	*anchor*
la cabina	*cabin*
la chimenea	*funnel*
el motor	*engine*
la popa	*stern*
la proa	*bows*
el puente	*bridge*
el radar	*radar*
el timón	*rudder*
las velas	*sails*
babor y estribor	*port and starboard*
el capitán	*captain*
el marinero	*sailor*
la niebla	*fog*
la sirena de niebla	*fog horn*
la tempestad	*gale*
la tripulación	*crew*

13 Los viajes y el turismo *Travel and tourism*

achicar	*to bail out*
echar vapor	*to steam*
gobernar	*to steer*
navegar	*to sail*
el bote salvavidas	*lifeboat*
el cinturón salvavidas	*lifebelt*
el embarque	*embarcation*
el iceberg	*iceberg*
el naufragio	*shipwreck*
ahogarse	*to drown*
chocar con una roca	*to hit a rock*
hundirse	*to sink*
nadar	*to swim*
naufragar	*to be shipwrecked*
rescatar	*to rescue*

En la playa *At the sea-side*

(See also *Hobbies and Sports*, page 117.)

las aletas	*flippers*
el alga	*seaweed*
la arena	*sand*
el bañador	*swimming costume*
la crema bronceadora	*sun cream*
la crema para después del sol	*after-sun cream*

el cubo y la pala	*bucket and spade*
la duna	*dune*
las gafas de sol	*sunglasses*
los guijarros	*shingle*
la loción para las quemaduras de sol	*sunburn lotion*
el mar	*sea*
la marea	*tide*
la marea alta	*high tide*
la marea baja	*low tide*
el pic-nic; la merienda	*picnic*
la playa	*beach*
la protección contra el viento	*wind break*
el protector solar	*sunblock*
el puesto de los helados	*ice-cream kiosk*
la sombrilla	*parasol*
la toalla	*towel*
el tubo de respiración	*snorkel*
la tumbona	*deck chair*
bañarse	*to swim*
hacer castillos de arena	*to build sandcastles*
relajarse; descansar	*to relax*
tomar el sol	*to sunbathe*

13 Los viajes y el turismo *Travel and tourism*

LOS COCHES Y EL AUTOMOVILISMO
CARS AND MOTORING

el accidente	*accident*
las carreteras	*roads*
las señales de tráfico /de carreteras	*road signs*

En el taller *At the garage*

Las piezas del coche y los accesorios	**Car parts and accessories**
los accesorios	*accessories*
el airbag	*airbag*
la aleta	*wing*
los asientos	*seats*
la baca	*roof / roof rack*
la batería	*battery*
las bombillas de repuesto	*spare bulbs*
el botiquín	*first aid kit*
las bujías	*spark plugs*
la caja de cambios	*gear box*
el capó	*bonnet*
la carrocería	*body*
el catalizador	*catalytic converter*
la cerradura	*lock*
el chasis	*chassis*
el claxon	*horn*
el coche	*car*
la correa del ventilador	*fanbelt*
el depósito de la gasolina	*petrol tank*
la dirección asistida	*power assisted steering*
el embrague	*clutch*
los faros	*head lamps*
los frenos	*brakes*
los frenos ABS	*ABS brakes*
el gato	*jack*
los guantes de plástico	*plastic gloves*
los intermitentes	*indicators*
el lavaparabrisas	*screen wash*
los limpiaparabrisas	*windscreen wipers*
las luces cortas	*dipped headlights*
las luces largas	*full beam*
las luces de posición	*side lights*
las llaves	*keys*
el maletero	*boot*
el motor	*engine*
el neumático	*tyre*
el parachoques	*bumper*
las piezas	*parts*
la puerta	*door*
el retrovisor	*wing mirror*
la rueda	*wheel*
el tapón de la gasolina	*petrol cap*
el triángulo señalizador	*warning triangle*
el tubo de escape	*exhaust pipe*
la velocidad/ la marcha	*gear*
la ventanilla	*window*
el volante	*steering wheel*
el coche automático	*automatic car*
el coche con puerta trasera	*hatch back*
el coche deportivo	*sports car*
fórmula uno	*formula 1*

13 Los viajes y el turismo *Travel and tourism*

Las prestaciones **Performance**
el consumo *fuel consumption*
la dirección *steering*
los frenos *braking*
la potencia
(en caballos) *horse power*
la velocidad *speed*

el tren/el túnel de
lavado de
coches *car wash*
la cera de coche *car wax*

el/la aprendiz-a de
conductor-a *learner driver*
la autoescuela *driving school*
el carnet de
conducir *driving licence*
el carnet de conducir
provisional *provisional licence*
el impuesto de
circulación *road tax*
la ITV *MOT*
el manual *manual*
el seguro ... *... insurance*
a terceros *third party*
a todo riesgo *comprehensive*

el accidente *accident*
la asistencia *assistance*
el atasco;
el embotella-
miento *traffic jam; hold up*
el auxilio *breakdown*
en carretera *assistance*
la avería *breakdown*
el choque
en cadena *pile up*
la colisión;
el choque *collision*

el pinchazo *puncture*
el RACE *AA / RAC*
(equivalent)
la reparación *repair*
el teléfono de *emergency*
emergencia *telephone*

Las carreteras y señales de tráfico
Roads and road signs

la autopista *motorway*
la autovía *dual carriageway*
la carretera
nacional *main road*
la calle de dirección
única *one-way street*
el callejón sin
salida *cul de sac*
la carretera
comarcal *country road*

el arcén *hard shoulder*
el bordillo *verge*
el carril *lane*
el carril de adelanta-
miento *overtaking lane*
la curva *bend*
el desvío *diversion*
el límite de
velocidad *speed restriction*
las obras de
carretera *road works*
el peaje *toll*
el semáforo *traffic lights*
las señales de
emergencia *emergency lights*

prohibido
adelantar *no overtaking*

13 Los viajes y el turismo *Travel and tourism*

En la estación de servico
At the services

el aceite	*oil*
el anti-	
congelante	*anti-freeze*
la bombilla	*light bulb*
la gasolina . . .	*. . . petrol*
con plomo	*leaded*
sin plomo	*unleaded*
súper	*four star*
el gas-oil	*diesel*
la gasolinera	*petrol station*
el líquido	
de frenos	*brake fluid*
el mapa de	
carreteras	*road map*
la presión de los	
neumáticos	*tyre pressure*
el surtidor de	
gasolina	*petrol pump*
la carta verde	*green card*

la documentación	
del coche	*car papers*
el seguro	*insurance*
adelantar	*to overtake*
atropellar	*to run over*
cambiar de	
velocidad	*to change gear*
chocar con	*to collide*
conducir	*to drive*
dar contra	*to hit*
dar marcha	
atrás	*to reverse*
derrapar	*to skid*
dirigir; manejar	*to steer*
exceder la velocidad	
permitida	*to speed*
frenar	*to brake*
perder el control	*to lose control*
quedarse sin	
gasolina	*to run out of petrol*
recalentar	*to overheat*
tener una	
avería	*to break down*
torcer	
(bruscamente)	*to swerve*

Expressiones útiles *Useful expressions*

¡Lleno, por favor!	*Fill her up!*
Mi coche no arranca	*My car won't start*
¿Puede comprobar . . .	*Could you check . . .*
el aceite	*the oil*
el agua	*the water*
la presión	*the tyre pressures?*
Me he quedado sin gasolina	*I've run out of petrol*
El motor se calienta mucho	*The engine's overheating*
¿Hay un taller de reparaciones	
cerca, por favor?	*Is there a garage near here, please?*
¿Arreglan pinchazos?	*Do you repair punctures?*
Quisiera alquilar un coche	*I'd like to hire a car*
¿Puedo pagar con tarjeta de crédito?	*Can I pay by credit card?*

EL CAMPO
THE COUNTRYSIDE

El paisaje *Landscape*

el campo	*country*
el pueblo	*village*
la iglesia	*church*
el arroyo	*stream*
la cascada	*waterfall*
el desierto	*desert*
el estanque	*pond*
el lago	*lake*
la llanura	*plain*
la marisma	*marsh*
el río	*river*
las rocas	*rocks*
el valle	*valley*
la colina	*hill*
la cumbre	*summit*
el funicular	*funicular*
la montaña	*mountain*
el pico	*mountain peak*
la sierra	*mountain range*
el teleférico	*cable railway*
el camino	*path*
la pradera	*grassland*
el prado	*field*
la puerta	*gate*
el sendero	*footpath*
el seto	*hedge*
la tapia	*wall*

Los árboles *Trees*

el bosque	*wood*
la selva	*forest*

Los árboles de hoja caduca **Deciduous trees**

el abedul	*silver birch*
el álamo	*poplar*
el alcornoque	*cork tree*
el arce	*maple*
el castaño	*chestnut*
el eucalipto	*eucalyptus*
el fresno	*ash*
la haya	*beech*
la magnolia	*magnolia*
el roble	*oak*
el sauce	*willow*
el sicomoro	*sycamore*

Los árboles coníferos **Coniferous trees**

el abeto	*fir*
el alerce	*larch*
el pino	*pine*

Los frutales **Fruit trees**

el aguacate	*avocado*
el albaricoquero	*apricot*
el almendro	*almond*
el ciruelo	*plum*
la higuera	*fig*
el limonero	*lemon*
el manzano	*apple*
el melocotonero	*peach*
el naranjo	*orange*
el olivo	*olive*
la palmera	*palm*
el peral	*pear*
andar; caminar	*to walk*
dar una caminata	*to hike*
dar una carrera; correr	*to go for a run*
montar en bicicleta	*to cycle*
montar a caballo	*to ride*
merendar en el campo	*to have a picnic*

¡OTRA VEZ!

● *Activity:* ¿Qué significan estos símbolos? *What do the symbols mean?*

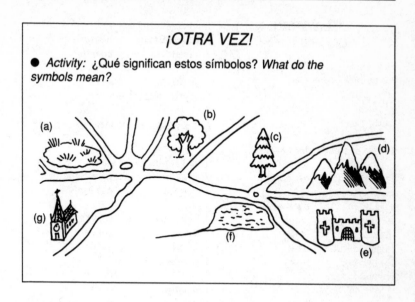

14 La naturaleza *The natural world*

EN LA GRANJA
ON THE FARM

la granja	*farm*
los edificios de la granja	*farm buildings*
el corral	*farm yard*
la tierra de labranza	*farm land*
la casa de campo	*farmhouse*
la agricultura	*arable farming*
el cobertizo; la nave	*shed*
la cuadra	*stable*
el establo	*stall*
la ganadería	*cattle*
los lácteos	*dairy*
el ganado vacuno	*beef*
el granero	*barn*

Los animales domésticos
Farm animals

el/la ternero-a	*calf*
el toro	*bull*
la vaca	*cow*
el asno	*donkey*
el caballo	*horse*
el caballo de tiro	*cart horse*
el/la mulo-a	*mule*
el poney	*pony*
el potro	*foal*
el semental	*stallion*
la yegua	*mare*
el carnero	*ram*
el cordero	*lamb*
la oveja	*sheep*
la cerda	*sow*

el cerdo	*pig*
el cochinillo	*piglet*
el verraco	*boar*
la cabra	*goat*
el cabrito; el chivo	*kid*

Las aves de corral *Poultry*

la gallina	*hen*
el gallo	*cockerel*
el pollo	*chicken*
el ansarino	*gosling*
el ganso	*gander*
la oca	*goose*
el patito	*duckling*
el pato	*duck*
el arado	*plough*
la cosechadora	*combine harvester*
el tractor	*tractor*
la avena	*oats*
la cebada	*barley*
el centeno	*rye*
el grano	*grain*
el heno	*hay*
el maíz	*corn*
la paja	*straw*
el trigo	*wheat*
la cerca	*fence*
el corral	*paddock*
cosechar	*to harvest*
cultivar	*to cultivate*
dar de comer a los animales	*to feed the animals*
plantar	*plant*
regar	*to irrigate*
sembrar	*to sow*

LOS ANIMALES
ANIMALS

la ardilla	*squirrel*
la comadreja	*weasel*
el conejo	*rabbit*
el gusano	*worm*
el hurón	*ferret*
la liebre	*hare*
el lobo	*wolf*
la mofeta	*skunk*

LA CAZA MAYOR Y OTROS MAMÍFEROS
BIG GAME AND OTHER MAMMALS

el antílope	*antelope*
la ballena	*whale*
el bisonte	*bison*
el búfalo	*buffalo*
el camello	*camel*
la cebra	*zebra*
el canguro	*kangaroo*
el chimpancé	*chimpanzee*
el ciervo	*reindeer*
el coala	*koala*
el delfín	*dolphin*
el elefante	*elephant*
la foca	*seal*
el gorila	*gorilla*
el hipopótamo	*hippopotamus*
la hiena	*hyena*
el jaguar	*jaguar*
el jabalí	*wild boar*
la jirafa	*giraffe*
el león	*lion*
el leopardo	*leopard*
el mono	*monkey*
el oso	*brown bear*

la nutria	*otter*
el puerco espín	*hedgehog*
la rana	*frog*
la rata	*rat*
el sapo	*toad*
el tejón	*badger*
el topo	*mole*
el visón	*mink*
el zorro	*fox*

la pantera	*panther*
el rinoceronte	*rhinoceros*
la serpiente	*snake*
el tigre	*tiger*

Las partes del cuerpo de un animal
Parts of the animal

las astas	*horns; antlers*
los bigotes	*whiskers*
el caparazón; la concha	*shell*
la cola	*tail*
el colmillo	*tusk*
la cornamenta	*antlers*
el cuerno	*horn*
la escama	*scale*
la giba	*hump*
el hocico	*snout*
la pata	*paw*
el pelo	*coat*
la pezuña	*hoof*
el pellejo	*skin*
la piel	*fur*
la púa	*spike*
la trompa	*trunk*
la zarpa	*claw*

LOS PÁJAROS; LAS AVES
BIRDS

el águila	*eagle*
el águila pescadora	*osprey*
el águila real	*golden eagle*
la agachadiza	*snipe*
la alondra	*skylark*
el avión	*martin*
el búho	*owl*
el buitre	*vulture*
la cigüeña	*stork*
el cisne	*swan*
el cormorán	*cormorant*
el cuco; el cuclillo	*cuckoo*
el cuervo	*crow*
el estornino	*starling*
el faisán	*pheasant*
el gavilán	*hawk*
la gaviota	*seagull*
la golondrina	*swallow*
el gorrión	*sparrow*
el grajo	*rook*
el halcón	*falcon*

el herrerillo	*blue-tit*
la lechuza	*barn owl*
el martín pescador	*kingfisher*
el mirlo	*blackbird*
la paloma	*dove*
el palomo; el pichón	*pigeon*
el pelícano	*pelican*
la perdiz	*partridge*
el petirrojo	*robin*
el pinzón	*chaffinch*
el ruiseñor	*nightingale*
la urraca	*magpie*
el vencejo	*swift*
el zorzal	*thrush*
el ala	*wing*
el huevo	*egg*
el nido	*nest*
el pico	*beak*
la pluma	*feather*
la zarpa; la uña	*claw*
la ornitología	*ornithology*
observar aves	*bird-watching*

INSECTOS
INSECTS

la abeja	*bee*
la colmena	*bee-hive*
el panal	*honey comb*
la miel	*honey*
la araña	*spider*
la tela de araña	*spider's web*
la avispa	*wasp*
el nido de avispa	*wasp's nest*

la cucaracha	*cockroach*
el grillo	*cricket*
el gusano	*grub; maggot*
la hormiga	*ant*
la libélula	*dragonfly*
la mariposa	*butterfly / moth*
la mariquita	*ladybird*
la mosca	*fly*
el mosquito	*mosquito*
la oruga	*caterpillar*
la pulga	*flea*
el saltamontes	*grasshopper*
el tábano	*horse fly*
la típula	*cranefly*

14 **La naturaleza** *The natural world*

cazar	*to hunt*	ladrar	*to bark*
la caza	*hunting*	maullar	*to miaow*
disparar	*to shoot*	mugir	*to moo*
		relinchar	*to neigh*
aullar	*to howl*	ronronear	*to purr*
balar	*to bleat*	rugir	*to roar*
cacarear	*to crow*	silbar	*to hiss*
gatear	*to crawl*	ulular	*to hoot*
gruñir	*to grunt*	zumbar	*to buzz*

Temas del medio ambiente
Environmental issues

el medio ambiente	*environment*
la contaminación	*environmental pollution*
el agujero en la capa de ozono	*hole in the ozone layer*
el alga tóxica	*toxic alga*
la biosfera	*biosphere*
el calentamiento global	*global warming*
la capa de ozono	*ozone layer*
los CFCs	*CFC's*
la contaminación del agua	*water pollution*
la contaminación del aire	*air pollution*
la contaminación urbana	*urban pollution*
la deforestación de la selva tropical	*destruction of the rain forest*
la desertización	*desertisation*
la destrucción del habitat	*destruction of the habitat*
la destrucción del medio ambiente	*destruction of the environment*
la ecología	*ecology*
los ecologistas	*ecologists*
el efecto invernadero	*greenhouse effect*
la erosión del suelo	*soil erosion*

los fertilizantes	*fertilizers*	el carbón	*coal*
la lluvia ácida	*acid rain*	la central	
la marea negra	*oil slick*	eléctrica	*power station*
la niebla tóxica	*smog*	la central	*nuclear power*
el Partido Verde	*Green Party*	nuclear	*station*
los pesticidas	*pesticides*	el combustible	*fuel*
la política verde	*green politics*	el combustible	
la protección		nuclear	*nuclear fuel*
medio-	*environmental*	el combustible	
ambiental	*protection*	sólido	*solid fuel*
los rayos		la energía	
ultravioletas	*ultraviolet rays*	nuclear	*nuclear power*
el reciclaje	*re-cycling*	la fusión	
los recursos		nuclear	*nuclear fusion*
naturales	*natural resources*	el gas	*gas*
el rescate		el petróleo	*oil*
de terrenos	*land reclamation*	la radiación	*radiation*
los residuos		los vertidos	
radioactivos	*radioactive waste*	nucleares	*nuclear waste*
la selva tropical	*rain forest*		
la super-			
población	*overpopulation*		

la energía ...	*... power / energy*
eólica	*wind*
hidroeléctrica	*hydroelectric*
de las mareas	*tidal*
solar	*solar*
las energías renovables	*renewable energy*
la protección de los animales	*protection of animals*
la protección del medio ambiente	*protection of the environment*

ahorrar	*to save*	destruir	*to destroy*
conservar	*to conserve*	malgastar	*to waste*
contaminar	*to contaminate;*	proteger	*to protect*
	pollute	reciclar	*to recycle*

14 La naturaleza *The natural world*

EL TIEMPO Y EL CLIMA
WEATHER AND THE CLIMATE

El tiempo *The weather*

el aire	*air*
la atmósfera	*atmosphere*
el barómetro	*barometer*
el calor	*heat*
el cielo	*sky*
el clima	*climate*
el frío	*cold*
la humedad	*humidity*
la precipitación	*rainfall*
el pronóstico (del tiempo)	*forecast*
la sequía	*drought*
el termómetro	*thermometer*
la visibilidad	*visibility*
el aguacero; el chaparrón	*downpour*
el aguanieve	*sleet*
el arco iris	*rainbow*
la brisa	*breeze*
el chubasco	*shower*
los claros	*bright intervals*
el granizo	*hail*
la helada	*frost*
el hielo	*ice*
la inundación	*flood*

la llovizna	*drizzle*
la lluvia	*rain*
el mal tiempo	*bad weather*
la neblina	*mist*
la niebla	*fog*
la nieve	*snow*
la bola de nieve	*snowball*
el muñeco de nieve	*snowman*
el quitanieves	*snowplough*
la nevada	*snowstorm*
la nube	*cloud*
la ola de calor/frío	*heat wave / cold snap*
la racha de viento	*gust*
el rocío	*dew*
el sol	*sun*
el torbellino	*whirlwind*
la tormenta	*storm*
el trueno y el relámpago	*thunder and lightning*
el viento	*wind*
de Levante	*East wind*
de Poniente	*West wind*
las altas presiones	*high pressure*
las bajas presiones	*low pressure*
la borrasca	*storm*
el frente cálido	*warm front*
la gota fría	*cold front*

Hace ...	It is ...
calor	*hot*
fresco	*cool*
frío	*cold*
humedad	*humid*
niebla	*foggy; misty*
viento	*windy*
buen tiempo	*fine*

173

14 **La naturaleza** *The natural world*

un tiempo lluvioso	*rainy*
un tiempo pesado	*heavy*
un tiempo seco	*dry*
un tiempo templado	*mild*
un tiempo variable	*changeable*
Está/estaba . . .	*It is / it was . . .*
granizando	*hailing*
helando	*freezing*
lloviendo	*raining*
nevando	*snowing*
nublado	*cloudy*
El cielo está . . .	*The sky is . . .*
azul	*blue*
cubierto	*overcast*
despejado	*clear*
nublado	*cloudy*
oscuro	*dark*

aclarar	*to clear up*	llover	*to rain*
cambiar	*to change*	mejorar	*to improve*
derretir	*to melt*	nevar	*to snow*
deshelar	*to thaw*		
granizar	*to hail*	Habrá . . .	*There will be . . .*
hacer calor	*to be hot*	chubascos	*showers*
hacer frío	*to be cold*	claros	*bright intervals*
hacer sol	*to be sunny*	fuertes vientos	*strong winds*
helar	*to freeze*	nieve	*snow*

15 El ancho mundo *The wide world*

EL MUNDO
THE WORLD

el Círculo Polar Antártico	*Antarctic Circle*
el Círculo Polar Ártico	*Arctic Circle*
el ecuador	*equator*
el globo	*the Globe*
la latitud	*latitude*
la longitud	*longitude*
la Tierra	*the Earth*
los trópicos	*the tropics*
el trópico de Capricornio	*Tropic of Capricorn*
el trópico de Cáncer	*Tropic of Cancer*

La brújula *The compass*

Norte	*North*
Sur	*South*
Este	*East*
Oeste	*West*

Los continentes
The continents

África	*Africa*
América	*America*
América del Norte	*North America*
Centroamérica	*Central America*
América del Sur	*South America*
Antártida	*Antarctica*
Asia	*Asia*
Europa	*Europe*
Oceanía	*Oceania*

Otros territorios
Other land masses

el Extremo/Lejano Oriente	*Far East*
la India	*India*
el Oriente Medio	*Middle East*

Los océanos *Oceans*

el Antártico	*Antarctic*
el Ártico	*Arctic*
el Atlántico	*Atlantic*
el Pacífico	*Pacific*
el Índico	*Indian*

Los mares *Seas*

el mar Adriático	*the Adriatic Sea*
Báltico	*Baltic Sea*
del Norte	*North Sea*
Mediterráneo	*Mediterranean*
Negro	*Black Sea*

el canal de la Mancha
the English Channel
el estrecho (de Gibraltar)
the Straits of Gibraltar

Los Países de Europa y la Unión Europea
The Countries of Europe and the European Union

país	*country*	adjetivo	*adjective*
Reino Unido	*United Kingdom*		
Gran Bretaña	*Great Britain*	británico-a	*British*
Inglaterra	*England*	inglés-esa	*English*
Gales	*Wales*	galés-esa	*Welsh*
Irlanda del Norte	*Northern Ireland*	irlandés-esa del Norte	*Northern Irish*
Irlanda	*Ireland*	irlandés-esa del Sur	*Irish*
Escocia	*Scotland*	escocés-esa	*Scottish*
Escandinavia	*Scandinavia*	escandinavo-a	*Scandinavian*
Dinamarca	*Denmark*	danés-esa	*Danish*
Finlandia	*Finland*	finlandés-esa	*Finnish*
Suecia	*Sweden*	sueco-a	*Swedish*
Noruega	*Norway*	noruego-a	*Norwegian*

Europa del Oeste   *Western Europe*

país	*country*	adjetivo	*adjective*
Bélgica	*Belgium*	belga	*Belgian*
Francia	*France*	francés-esa	*French*
Alemania	*Germany*	alemán-ana	*German*
Holanda	*Holland*	holandés-esa	*Dutch*
Hungría	*Hungary*	húngaro-a	*Hungarian*
Italia	*Italy*	italiano-a	*Italian*
Luxemburgo	*Luxembourg*	luxemburgués-esa	*Luxembourgish*
Portugal	*Portugal*	portugués-esa	*Portuguese*
España	*Spain*	español-a	*Spanish*
Suiza	*Switzerland*	suizo-a	*Swiss*

Europa Central   *Central Europe*

país	*country*	adjetivo	*adjective*
Austria	*Austria*	austríaco-a	*Austrian*
Bosnia	*Bosnia*	bosnio-a	*Bosnian*
Bulgaria	*Bulgaria*	búlgaro-a	*Bulgarian*
Croacia	*Croatia*	croata	*Croat*
Polonia	*Poland*	polaco-a	*Polish*
Eslovaquia	*Slovakia*	eslovaco-a	*Slovak*
Eslovenia	*Slovenia*	esloveno-a	*Slovene*

Grecia	*Greece*	griego-a	*Greek*
Rumania	*Romania*	rumano-a	*Rumanian*
Rusia	*Russia*	ruso-a	*Russian*
la República Checoslovaca	*Czech Republic*	checo-a	*Czech*
Turquía	*Turkey*	turco-a	*Turkish*

América Latina	*Latin America*		
Argentina	*Argentina*	argentino-a	*Argentinian*
Bolivia	*Bolivia*	boliviano-a	*Bolivian*
Brasil	*Brazil*	brasileño-a	*Brazilian*
Chile	*Chile*	chileno-a	*Chilean*
Colombia	*Colombia*	colombiano-a	*Colombian*
Costa Rica	*Costa Rica*	costarricense	*Costa Rican*
Cuba	*Cuba*	cubano-a	*Cuban*
Ecuador	*Ecuador*	ecuatoriano-a	*Ecuadorian*
El Salvador	*El Salvador*	salvadoreño-a	*Salvadorian*
Guatemala	*Guatemala*	guatemalteco-a	*Guatemalan*
Haití	*Haiti*	haitiano-a	*Haitian*
Honduras	*Honduras*	hondureño-a	*Honduran*
México	*Mexico*	mejicano-a	*Mexican*
Nicaragua	*Nicaragua*	nicaragüense	*Nicaraguan*
Panamá	*Panama*	panameño-a	*Panamanian*
Paraguay	*Paraguay*	paraguayo-a	*Paraguayan*
Perú	*Peru*	peruano-a	*Peruvian*
República Dominicana	*Dominican Republic*	dominicano-a	*Dominican*
Uruguay	*Uruguay*	uruguayo-a	*Uruguayan*
Venezuela	*Venezuela*	venezolano-a	*Venezuelan*

Nationalities

Formed by adjective (without article)

Soy inglés.	*I am English / an Englishman.*
Es española.	*She is Spanish / a Spaniard.*
Los ingleses	*The English*

15 El ancho mundo *The wide world*

Languages

Where appropiate, formed by masculine form of adjective

Hablo italiano.	*I speak Italian.*
Se habla inglés	*English spoken*
¿Hablas francés?	*Do you speak French?*

¡OTRA VEZ!

● *Activity: How many of the EU countries can you name in Spanish?*

15 **El ancho mundo** *The wide world*

ORGANISMOS NACIONALES E INTERNACIONALES
NATIONAL AND INTERNATIONAL AGENCIES

Organismos nacionales
National organisations

CEPYME	*small business confederation*
Iberia	*state airline*
INI	*national institute for industry*
ONCE	*national blind association*
RACE	*Spanish RAC*
RENFE	*state railways*
RNE	*state radio*
TVE	*state television*

La Unión Europea
The European Union

el Presidente	*The President*
el Consejo de Europa	*Council of Europe*

Organismos internacionales
World organisations

las Naciones Unidas	*United Nations*
la Organización Mundial de la Salud (OMS)	*World Health Organisation*
la Cruz Roja	*Red Cross*
la OTAN	*NATO*
Greenpeace	*Greenpeace*
el FMI	*International Monetary Fund*

15 El ancho mundo *The wide world*

NOTICIAS INTERNACIONALES
INTERNATIONAL NEWS ITEMS

el corresponsal	*correspondant*
las noticias	*news*
el accidente	*accident*
el accidente de aviación	*plane crash*
el alud; la avalancha	*avalanche*
el ciclón	*cyclone*
la colisión de trenes	*train crash*
el corrimiento; el desprendimiento de tierras	*landslide*
el desastre	*disaster*
la epidemia	*epidemic*
la erupción de volcán	*volcano eruption*
la explosión de bomba	*bomb explosion*
el golpe de estado	*coup*
la guerra	*war*
la guerra civil	*civil war*
el hambre	*famine*
el hundimiento	*collapse*
el huracán	*hurricane*
el incendio	*fire*
la inundación	*flood*
la invasión	*invasion*
la ola de calor	*heatwave*
la peste	*plague*
la sequía	*drought*
el terremoto	*earthquake*
el terrorismo	*terrorism*
el tifón	*typhoon*
el tornado	*tornado*

conmocionado/a	*shocked*
herido/a	*wounded*
quemado/a	*burned*
el rehén	*hostage*
el/la superviviente	*survivor*
la víctima	*victim*
escribir; redactar	*to write*
imprimir	*to print*
morir; fallecer	*to die*
ser asesinado-a	*to be assassinated / murdered*
ser herido-a; sufrir heridas	*to be injured*
ser matado-a/ muerto-a (por)	*to be killed (by)*

Titulares de noticias internacionales
International news headlines

31 intoxicados por humo en el metro de Londres

■ **Manifestación de la oposición en México**

■ **Nace un nuevo grupo guerrillero en Colombia**

Accidente en un crucero británico

15 El ancho mundo *The wide world*

EL ESPACIO
SPACE

el agujero negro	*black hole*
el año luz	*light year*
el asteroide	*asteroid*
el/la astronauta	*astronaut*
el cometa	*comet*
la constelación	*constellation*
el/la cosmon-	
auta	*cosmonaut*
el cosmos	*cosmos*
el eclipse	*eclipse*
la estación	
espacial	*space station*
la estrella	*star*
el extraterrestre	*alien*
la galaxia	*galaxy*
la luna	*moon*
el meteoro	*meteor; meterorite*
la nave espacial	*spacecraft;*
	spaceship
la nebulosa	*nebula*
el OVNI	*UFO*

el planeta	*planet*
el satélite	*satellite*
el telescopio	*telescope*
el transbordador	
espacial	*shuttle*
el universo	*universe*
la velocidad de	
la luz/del	
sonido	*speed of light / sound*
la Vía Láctea	*Milky Way*
orbitar	*to circle; orbit*

Los planetas *The planets*

Júpiter	*Jupiter*
Marte	*Mars*
Mercurio	*Mercury*
Neptuno	*Neptune*
Plutón	*Pluto*
Saturno	*Saturn*
la Tierra	*Earth*
Urano	*Uranus*
Venus	*Venus*

Los daños son de 20.000 millones de dólares

El huracán «Andrés» va perdiendo violencia al adentrarse en Louisiana

Balance de 17 muertos a su paso por EEUU

16 *Extras*

Sr.	*Mr*
Sra.	*Mrs*
Srta.	*Miss*
D.	*Don*
Dña.	*Doña.*
Dr.	*Doctor (male)*
Dra.	*Doctor (female)*
Dtor.	*Director (male)*
Dtora.	*Director (female)*
Ldo.	*for a graduate (male)*
Lda.	*graduate (female)*
ej.	*e.g.*
C/	*calle*
Av.	*Avenida*
dcha.	*right*
izqda.	*left*
Rte.	*sender (on back of envelope)*
EE.UU	*Estados Unidos*
pta., ptas.	*peseta(s)*
IVA	*VAT*

The first letter or two letters of Spanish car registration numbers correspond to the province in which the care were registered. These are:

AB	Albacete	LU	Lugo
AL	Almería	M	Madrid
AV	Avila	MA	Málaga
B	Barcelona	ML	Melilla
BA	Badajoz	MU	Murcia
BI	Bilbao	NA	Navarra
BU	Burgos	O	Oviedo
CA	Cádiz	OR	Orense
CC	Cácares	P	Palencia
CE	Ceuta	PM	Palma de Mallorca
CO	Córdoba	PO	Pontevedra
CR	Ciudad Real	S	Santander
CS	Castellón	SA	Salamanca
CU	Cuenca	SE	Sevilla
GC	Gran Canaria	SG	Segovia
GE	Gerona	SS	San Sebastián
GR	Granada	T	Tarragona
GU	Guadalajara	TF	Tenerife
H	Huelva	TO	Toledo
HU	Huesca	V	Valencia
J	Jaén	VA	Valladolid
LE	León	Z	Zaragoza
LO	Logroño	ZA	Zamora

16 *Extras*

SLANG AND EXPLETIVES

You are advised not to use this language yourself as it is likely to give offence, but you may find it useful to be able to understand it!

It is especially difficult for a non-native speaker to judge when slang can be used, how much offence it is likely to give and what reaction it is likely to bring on. Ask yourself how you would react to being sworn at by a foreigner and try to find other ways of responding.

Expressions of anger/frustration/surprise

¡Joder!
¡Coño!
¡Mierda!

Insulting people

¡Cabrón!
¡Maricón!
¡Gilipollas!
¡Vete a la mierda!
¡Hijo de puta!

Expressions of enthusiasm/disgust

¡Es de puta madre!   *(enthusiasm)*
¡Qué asco!   *(disgust)*

PERDONE, POR FAVOR
EXCUSE ME, PLEASE

¡Socorro!; ¡Auxilio!	*Help!*
¿Habla inglés?	*Do you speak English?*
¡Disculpe! ¡Perdone!	*Sorry! Pardon!*
Lo siento.	*I'm sorry.*
¿Cómo?	*Pardon?*
No comprendo.	*I don't understand.*
¿Puede repetirlo, por favor?	*Can you repeat that please*
Más despacio, por favor	*Can you say it more slowly?*
¿Qué quiere decir eso en inglés?	*What does that mean in English?*
¿Habla . . . ?	*Do you speak . . . ?*
¿Cómo se escribe . . . ?	*How do you spell . . . ?*
¿Puede escribirme eso, por favor?	*Can you write that down for me please?*
¿Puede ayudarme?	*Can you help me?*
¿Comprende?	*Do you understand?*
Por favor.	*Please.*
Gracias.	*Thank you.*
De nada.	*Don't mention it.*
¡Oiga!	*Listen!*

16 *Extras*

Lo siento, no he querido molestarle	*I'm sorry, I did not mean to give offence.*
Lo siento, he entendido mal.	*Sorry, I misunderstood.*
Me temo que no me ha entendido bien.	*I'm afraid you have misunderstood me.*

Ha sido culpa mía.	*It was my fault.*	Aviso	*Warning*
		Peligro	*Danger*
NO ha sido culpa mía	*It was NOT my fault.*	¡Ojo!	*Watch out!*
		¡Cuidado!	*Be careful!*
Ha sido culpa suya.	*It was your fault.*	Peligroso	*Dangerous*

SERVICIOS DE EMERGENCIAS
EMERGENCY SERVICES

la Guardia Civil	*Civil Guard*	los Bomberos	*Fire Brigade*
la Policía Local	*Local Police*	Cruz Roja	*Red Cross*
Protección Civil	*Civil Defence*	Urgencias S.S.	*Ambulance*